BLACK EXPLORERS

C. R. Gibbs
Three Dimensional Publishing
Silver Spring, Maryland

BLACK EXPLORERS
Copyright
1992, 1993, 1994, 1995, 1996, 1997, 1998

<u>First Edition</u>
First printing
Second Printing
Third Printing
Fourth Printing

Three Dimensional Publishing
1015 Stirling Road
Silver Spring, Maryland 20901
301-593-6450
Website: http://www.erols.com/tdpedu - E-Mail: tdpedu@erols.com

ISBN No. 1-877835-95-1

CONTENTS

Acknowledgments

My special thanks for the support and encouragement I received from: Daud Malik Watts, who first told me about Benjamin Anderson; Lawrence Jackson, Jerome Davis, Debrah Harris-Johnson, Dexter Akinsheye, and especially to Bettie Robinson for her patience and enthusiasm.

Foreword

This book is a primer on black exploration. Its purpose is to centralize available information on black explorers and serve as a springboard for additional research on the subject. Each of the book's five chapters offers information on a different aspect of the involvement of blacks in the exploration of Africa, the Americas, the polar regions, and other parts of the world.

Chapter One, Portal to Adventure, highlights major African figures in the independent exploration of the continent by indigenous Africans. The emphasis in this chapter is on blacks who planned, directed, and performed explorations inside Africa for purposes of trade, diplomacy, adventure, or curiosity. The popular notion of an African explorer is usually a native rifle bearer or porter; a black man or woman in any of a variety of subservient roles. Individuals in Chapter One go against the traditional limited images of Africans.

By emphasizing Africans who explored Africa on their own, I do not seek to disparage the memory of those who aided European and Arab explorers. But, even these Africans need to be viewed as more than appendages to better known explorers. A few of these Africans left posterity fascinating records of their own feelings about their roles in the European exploration of their lands. Dorugu, who saw service with Adolf Overweg and Heinrich Barth, shared his recollections with J.F. Schon. They were published about the time Dorugu returned to Africa in the 1860s.

My choice to forego recounting the contributions of these Africans unfortunately omits the virtually untouched area of black female African explorers. Although I did not locate any African women who took part in planning or commanding expeditions in Africa (with the exception of Hatshepsut who is mentioned in Chapter Two), a number of African women accompanied the expeditions in which their husbands served. During his travels in Africa between 1866 and 1871, Livingstone was accompanied by such women. They gamely shared every hardship their husbands did. These are potential subjects for a subsequent book on black explorers.

The historical record demonstrates conclusively that Africans were the first to explore their own continent. Chapter One provides names and exploits of several individuals who explored the land and waters of Africa as far back as 2300 B.C. and served in positions of leadership.

Chapter Two, the Ancient Maritime Heritage of Africa, shows how much Africans were wedded to the concept of water travel; the only way other than by foot to cover great distances. From crude papyrus rafts on the Nile to great riverine war canoes nearly as long as Spanish caravels, the diversity and history of African maritime enterprise is surveyed. In instance after instance, the chapter demonstrates that Africans had the motive, means, and opportunities for long distance ocean travel. Chapter Two also describes how that African seafaring skill soon brought blacks into contact with European sea power and the events which followed.

Chapter Three, The African Exploration of America, relates the various ways in which Africans came to the Americas. First, they came as independent seafarers. Some may have settled where they first sighted landfall. Traces of these men were still there when the first

European explorers arrived. Thousands of blacks came as explorers and pioneers with the Europeans. Many of them were free black men from Spain and did not come directly from Africa as slaves. Those came later and in greater numbers. Chapter Three also describes the alliances between native Americans and Africans to resist enslavement and oppression. This chapter covers a broad canvas and provides examples of those various situations drawn from North, Central, South America, and the Caribbean.

Chapter Four, To Every Corner of the Earth, outlines black prehistoric and some later migrations to places outside Africa. Brief descriptions of African communities in Asia and on the islands of the Pacific are given. Of particular note is the presence of Africans in an area of the Pacific known as Melanesia. There is evidence to suggest that these prehistoric migrations were far more than random journeys. In the case of the Melanesians, they developed systems of navigation that took them precisely where they wanted to go. With this information, the reader can look afresh at the variety of ways in which peoples of supposedly less developed cultures have used their natural skills to achieve impressive scientific results. Chapter Four further demonstrates that blacks have, like the rest of the human race, been restless, footloose, and rugged; the very virtues needed to conquer mountains, cross seas, and span prairies.

Chapter Five, Exploring New Horizons, opens with the little known role of Africans in astronomy and astrology in ancient times. This chapter briefly covers the new crop of black explorers -- the astronauts. From Arnaldo Tamayo Mendez, the first black man in space, to Dr. Mae C. Jemison, the newest African American astronaut, the role of blacks in the exploration of the final frontier is described.

I have worked for a readable text without excessive documentation, trusting that references in the text will be adequate substantiation for this historical information. Those interested in pursuing further research may consult the bibliography included in this book.

The 19th Century, white historian Francis Parkman once wrote, that ''The history of Arctic and African travel... were... standing evidence that a trained and developed mind is not the enemy, but the active and powerful ally, of constitutional hardihood.'' Perhaps in the final analysis, the common trait — that links the early African explorer with today's African American astronaut and them to any other explorer — is not so much hardihood as much as strength, restlessness or even relentlessness. What all explorers possess after all, is that special light in the heart and mind, an enduring need to know.

Dedicated To The Africans:

Issaco, Susi, Chuma, and all the others who played pivotal roles in the exploration of Africa and whose courage, skill, and resourcefulness exemplify the best of the human character.

CHAPTER 1

PORTAL TO ADVENTURE:
THE BLACK EXPLORERS OF AFRICA

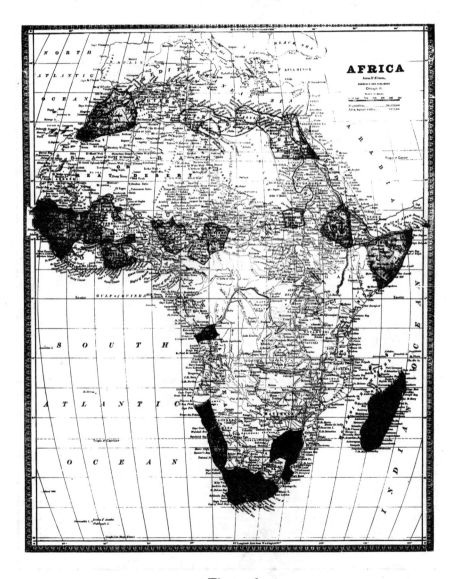

Figure 1

Nineteenth Century map of Africa

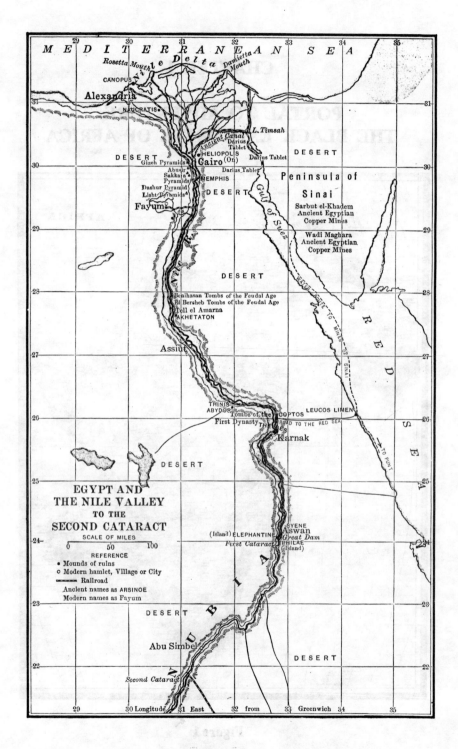

Figure 2

An 1884 map of Northeastern Africa

HARKHUF

On a sandy, windswept ridge at a place the Arabs call Qubbet al Hawa, across the Nile from the city of Aswan, lie the Tombs of the Nobles. Steps have been cut into the face of the ridge enabling you to make the steep climb up from the desert floor. At the top of this ancient staircase are a series of holes cut long ago into the rock. These rock cut tombs are the final resting places for Egyptian nobles who died four thousand years ago. Carved into the wall of one of the tombs is one of the earliest and most complete accounts of exploration undertaken by any major civilization. It is the story of an African explorer. He was an Egyptian nobleman called Harkhuf. He lived during the sixth dynasty of ancient Egypt c.2350 B.C.

Harkhuf was a man of many responsibilities. He called himself "Prince, seal bearer of the King of Lower Egypt, unique friend, lector-priest, god's seal bearer and confidant of royal commands." He was also Keeper of the Gateway of the South, a governor or viceroy of the region of southern Egypt and northern Sudan called Nubia. The region was the major source of Egyptian gold and Nubians were recruited to serve as police, archers, and infantry in the Egyptian army.

Harkhuf led several expeditions upriver well beyond the first cataract of the Nile River and deep into Nubia. His major objective was to establish peaceful trade with the local people. On two trips, he went with a military escort "to open up the way" and demonstrate his peaceful intentions.

Local Nubian rulers may have controlled trade with Egypt during this period or at least, according to some historians, are believed to have collected tolls on the goods that passed through their domains.

Harkhuf was a good businessman. On his third trip, he crossed back into Egyptian territory at the southern border at Elephantine with a convoy of three hundred donkeys bearing incense, ebony, panther skins, ivory, and "every good product."

Harkhuf returned from his fourth expedition with a most unusual item in addition to his usual cargo. He brought back "a dancing dwarf from the land of ghosts." As usual he sent a report of his journey written on papyrus scrolls by ship far down the Nile to the king at Memphis, the capital. He did not expect the king's scribe to write him the following reply:

> I have noted the content of your letter which you have sent to the king to make known your safe return from the land of Yam with your armed force... In this letter you say that you have brought a dancing dwarf of the god from the land of spirits, like the dwarf that the divine treasurer Ba-wr-dd brought from Pwnt in the time of King Issi. You say, "Never before has the like of him been brought by anyone else who has visited Yam."

King Issi was one of the last kings of the fifth dynasty. Pwnt is an interesting reference to the land of Punt or Puanit in East Africa and suggests regular seagoing trade between Egypt and East Africa.

The royal interest in the dwarf, probably a pygmy, may be related to the sacred status accorded them in Egyptian religious rites. The Egyptian god Bes, the personification of joy is believed to be based upon a pygmy type. The term *pygmy* is actually a misnomer. The word itself is of Greek origin and is the name for a race of dwarves described by ancient Greek writers. A more ethnologically correct name would be Twa, an African name for many of the small black peoples of Equatorial Africa.

The new young King Pepy II was eager to see the dwarf and ordered Harkhuf to bring him at once the nearly five hundred miles to Memphis:

> Come north to the court immediately and bring with you this dwarf that you have brought alive, healthy, and in good state from the land of spirits, for the god's dances, to rejoice the heart of the king, lord of Upper and lower Egypt, Nofr-ka-Ra, living forever. When he enters into your ship, set excellent people to be beside him on either hand, and take care that he does not fall into the water. When he is asleep at night, set excellent people to sleep beside him under the canopy, and do you yourself make ten inspections every night. My Majesty desires to see this dwarf more than all the gifts of Sinai and of Pwnt. If you arrive at court with this dwarf alive, healthy, and in good condition, my Majesty will do more for you than was done for the divine treasurer Ba-wr-dd in the time of Issi, such is my Majesty's desire to behold this dwarf.

Harkhuf was sufficiently proud of the royal summons to place it in his "house for eternity," his tomb. He was, he believed "more excellent, more vigilant than any count, companion, or caravan conductor who had been to Yam before." He wanted his honors and achievements to be spoken of long after he had gone to the blessed fields of his heaven. Harkhuf achieved a kind of immortality in another way, since much of the ancient trail blazed by him and his contemporaries is still in use today.

Harkhuf's primary trading destination was the Land of Yam, a large territory somewhere near the third cataract of the Nile. The cataracts are a series of rapids, acting as barriers to ships on the Nile between Elephantine and Meroe, one of the capitals of the kingdom of Kush in Nubia.

Harkhuf started from Aswan by the desert road on the west bank of the Nile and is believed to have reached Darfur and Kordofan in what is now Western Sudan. As R.W. Davis notes in an essay on black exploration in *The Negro Impact on Western Civilization*:

> The road to Darfur became a well-worn one thereafter. The track which leaves the Nile near Aswan to strike out the direction of Darfur is known today as the Elephantine Road, and as it enters the area of the desert between Darfur and the Nile Valley it becomes the Darb al-Arba'in, or Forty Days' Road along which thousands of caravans have passed, following the trail blazed by such men as Harkhuf.

Today, thousands of camels are herded along this same ancient road. There is a busy camel trade between Egypt and the Sudan that requires 50,000 camels each year to be driven north from Al-Nahud, Sudan through a nearly featureless desert to Bimban, Egypt. Some camels are then trucked farther north to Cairo.

As in Harkhuf's time, the majority of the men on these expeditions are hardy lean blacks who know the desert well. Like western cowboys they carry guns and saddles, eat their meals over blazing campfires, but at trail's end their celebrations are low key because they are Muslims and no drinking is permitted. Their wages are low. The work is risky. But the herders are stoic about their lives under an open desert sky.

Harkhuf, Pyopi-nakht, Ba-wr-dd and the other unknown, unnamed African explorers who "opened the way" set in motion events that touch us today. And they provide ancient proof that Africans were the first to explore Africa.

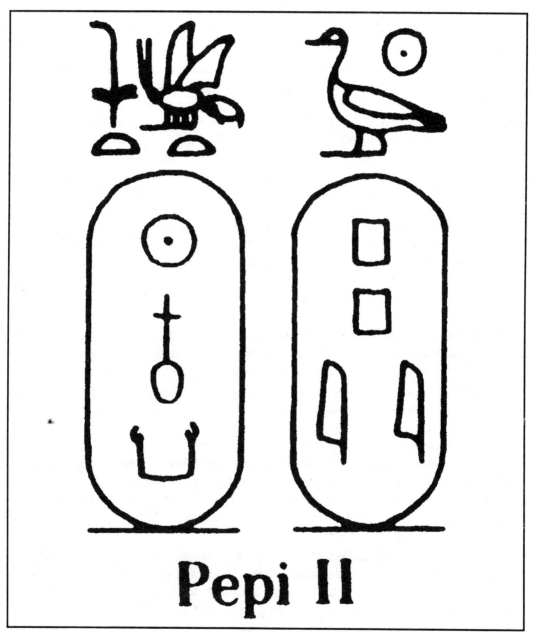

Figure 3

Cartouches of Pepi II. Each cartouche contains a name of the Pharoah.

Necho and Hanno

Pharaoh Necho II (610-595 B.C.) of the twenty-sixth dynasty of Egypt was one of the last native rulers of that ancient land. Often called a "merchant prince" because of his concern for trade, this northern Egyptian hoped to use the wealth from trade to bring stability and peace to the "Black Land." The original name for Egypt was Kemet which means the black land.

Necho ordered the construction of a canal from the Nile to the Red Sea. Necho also ordered and achieved the circumnavigation of the continent of Africa. An Egyptian, Peduneit, led the voyage. The Greek historian Herodotus, known as the "Father of History" reported the event one hundred fifty years later in Book IV of his *The Histories*:

> Libya, (Africa) shows that it has sea all round except the part that borders on Asia, Necho a king of Egypt being the first within our knowledge to show this fact; for when he stopped digging the canal which stretches from the Nile to the Arabian Gulf he sent forth Phoenician men in ships, ordering them to pull back between the Pillars of Heracles until they came to the Northern" (Mediterranean) "Sea and thus Egypt. The Phoenicians therefore setting forth from the Red Sea sailed in the Southern Sea" (Arabian Sea and Indian Ocean). "and whenever autumn came, they each time put ashore and sowed the land wherever they might be in Libya as they voyaged, and awaited the reaping-time; having then reaped the corn they set sail, so that after the passing of two years they doubled the Pillars of Heracles in the third year and came to Egypt. And they told things believable perhaps for others but unbelievable for me, namely that in sailing round Libya they had the sun on the right hand. Thus was Libya known for the first time.

Herodotus did not believe the story but it has the ring of truth. Historians have verified that the position of the sun would change during a circumnavigation of Africa, from east to west. There have also been some supporting archeological finds.

Another African with a thirst for distant markets or distant shores nearly accomplished the same feat again just a few years later. He has left history a record of his adventures. His name was Hanno. He was from the city of Carthage. In *African Glory*, J.C. DeGraft-Johnson describes Carthage "...the epitome of grandeur and pomp. It contained several imposing temples, a fortress, and many magnificent buildings. It was encircled by a triple line of fortification which secured it against all comers... If one included the suburbs as part of the city, its circumference was twenty-three miles. Its population numbered more than 70,000." Johnson is describing Carthage of northern Africa three hundred years before the birth of Christ.

Carthage was the leading sea power of its day. Its ships ranged across the Mediterranean Sea and out into the Atlantic in search of trade and wealth. Carthage often established colonies of its citizens in far away locations to develop commerce with local peoples and to serve as rendezvous or staging areas for its prowling fleets.

Around 530 B.C. Hanno, an admiral, was ordered to take a fleet of sixty 50-oared ships and 3,000 colonists and establish settlements on the coast of West Africa. A Greek version of the official report of his voyage originally written in Punic begins "Voyage of Hanno, King of the Carthaginians to the Afric lands beyond the Pillar of Heracles," an account of which he dedicated in the sanctuary of Baal, as follows (as translated by Paul Hermann in his book, *Conquest by Man*):

> We had now been sailing for four days and throughout each night we saw the land full of flames; in the midst of them was a very tall flame that towered above the other flames and seemed to reach up to the stars. By day we saw that it was a very high mountain. We named it the Chariot of the Gods (Mount Cameroon). When we had sailed along beside streams of fire for three days, we came to a gulf called the Southern Horn. In the depths of this bay lay an island. Upon it was a lake and in the lake an island peopled by crowds of savages. Most of them were women with rough, hairy bodies. Our interpreter called them gorillas. We pursued them. We could not catch the males; they escaped by flight. They were able to leap away over the rocks and kept us at bay with stones. Three of the females, who absolutely refused to follow, defended themselves against our men so violently by biting and scratching when we captured them, that we killed them. We then flayed them and bought back their skins with us to Carthage. As we had come to an end of our provisions, we did not continue our journey any farther.

Hanno embarked on this journey after safely establishing six settlements on the coast of Africa between what is now Morocco and Senegal. It was his curiosity that drove him on. Some historians have speculated that he was also trying to copy what Pharaoh Necho's fleet had done years earlier. Whatever his motives, Hannos' curiosity and courage compelled him to go on what is estimated to be a 6,250 mile roundtrip voyage of settlement and exploration, not achieved again for nearly two thousand years.

In *Civilization or Barbarism*, the late Dr. Cheik Anta Diop adds additional dimensions to the voyage of Hanno:

> Finally let us interpret a Senegalese oral tradition to which no attention has ever been paid, and which, in our opinion, would militate for a Carthaginian presence in antiquity on the Senegalese shores: this would be a strong confirmation of Hanno's expedition.

> It is said that Barka was Ndiadjan Ndiaye's brother and that his mother, Farimata Sall, Lam Toro's daughter, was of the Peul race of the Belianke. It is from his name, Barka, that came the word "Barka," or "Barak," designating the king of Walo, a region of the Senegal River's estuary, which the Carthaginians sailed (according to the very controversial interpretation of some Roman historical documents) to Bambuk, near Kaarta. There is in this story a constellation of Carthaginian names that may not be a matter of chance; but only well-conducted excavations all along the Senegal River up to the Kaarta country could one day confirm this hypothesis, with the discovery of characteristically Punic objects.

> In fact, Barka is not of Arabic origin; it is Carthaginian and it designates the royalty there where the Carthaginians had landed, if they ever came to

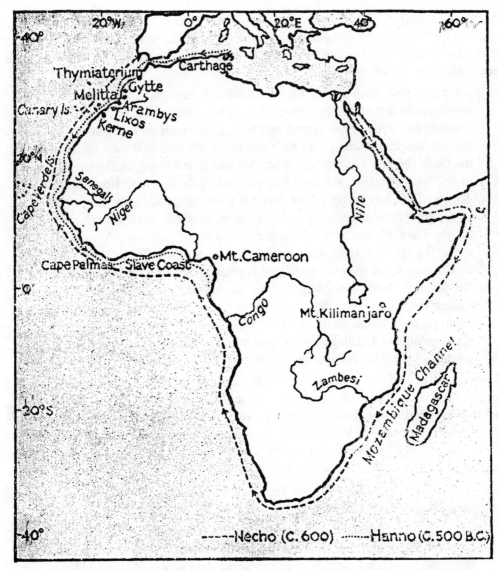

Figure 4

The African voyages of Necho and Hanno

Senegal. Belianke is a compound term which, in the Peul or even the Soninke languages, breaks down as follows: Bel + nke = the men of Bel or Bal (Punic god). And we know that Bal is still today a proper name of the Tukulors, the ethnic group that lives in the river region above. Kaarta is practically the exact term that the Carthaginians used to designate their town, which the Romans called Carthago, or Carthage.

According to the controversial text of Hanno's long and complicated journey, the Carthaginians supposedly left a colony (sixty persons or thirty couples) on Cerne Island, which is a strip of land near the Senegal

River estuary. The term Belianke, formed in the same manner as Soninke, Malinke, Foutanke, etc., necessarily precedes Islam and goes back to the sixth century B.C. during the time when the cult of Baal was still in force.

Diop believed that Carthaginian colonists had mixed with the coastal peoples of Senegal leaving traces of their religion and culture that remain today.

King Juba

King Juba was a scholar, explorer, and geographer who lived in North Africa while it was under Roman rule. He was born around 40 B.C. in the Roman province of Numidia. He was the second and younger of the two kings of Numidia named Juba.

As a child, he was taken to Rome by Julius Caesar. Taught to speak Latin and immersed in Roman law, science, and culture Juba became a Romanized African. However, he still maintained the ability to speak and read his native Punic. During this period he became friends with a man who later served as his mentor. His name was Gauis Julius Caesar Octavianus. Octavian as he was known, became impressed with Juba's eagerness to learn and the hard work he put into his studies. Juba's value increased to Rome in 46 B.C. when his father, the king, died. Juba was the heir to the throne of Numidia, a rich and fertile country which exported great quantities of wheat and olive oil to every corner of the Roman empire.

It was Juba's desire to know the world around him that brought him his greatest fame. He prowled the libraries reading everything he could find on sailing and geography. Juba talked to the captains of ships docked at the local Roman ports. He interviewed lowly sailors from all parts of the Roman dominion. The Roman writer Avenius described Juba as one of the most learned men of his day. Plutarch and Athenaeus also praised his learnedness. Juba is said to have influenced the writings of Seneca, a Roman statesman and philosopher.

In 30 B.C. Octavian emerged victorious from a war among rivals for the throne of the assassinated Julius Caesar. He defeated Mark Antony and Cleopatra, brought Egypt under Rome's heel, and formally established the Roman empire. He took the title Emperor Augustus.

Numidia, once an enemy of Rome while it fought Hannibal and then an ally of Rome against the African general, was returned to Juba by Augustus. Juba told Augustus, he wanted to trade Numidia for the larger neighboring county of Mauretania. Augustus complied. Perhaps Juba made the strange request because Mauretania was closer to the Atlantic Ocean. The mysteries of that vast expanse challenged him, even mocked him. He had to grasp its secrets. He held his dreams while he finished the work for which he became famous throughout the empire and was still being cited and studied by geographers until the nineteenth century.

Juba published a geography of Africa. It was a history or description of the continent. Juba's work described major topographical features as well as a large number of animals. The impact of the book was widespread and deep. Pliny the Elder cites Juba's work in his *Historica Naturalis*. Juba was clearly familiar with the coast of Africa from the Pillars of Hercules (Straits of Gibraltar) to Bab el Mandeb, a strait between Arabia and Africa connecting the Red Sea and the Gulf of Aden. This was a distance of over 3,000 kilometers or 1,800 miles. His work, assembled in part from ancient Carthaginian and Greek records, brought together an impressive array of data and revealed to the world his extraordinary degree of knowledge.

He developed an astounding theory, the first of its kind, about the origin of the Nile River. Juba believed that the Nile began inside a mountain in Western Mauretania near the

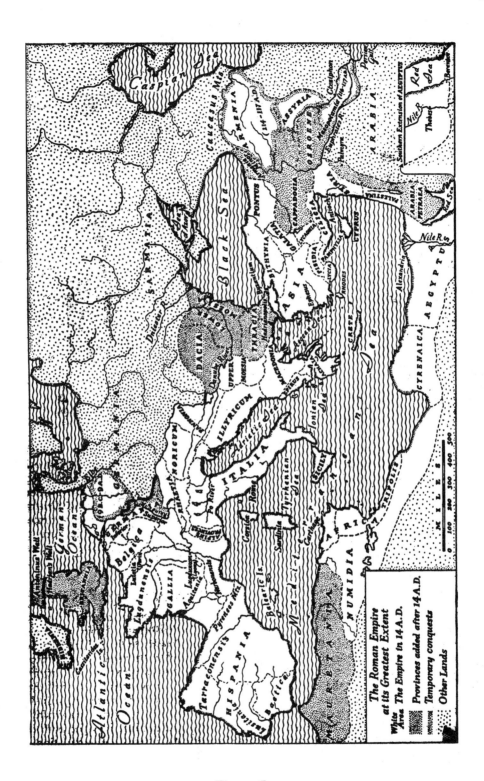

Figure 5

Northwestern Africa around the time of King Juba

Atlantic Ocean. Nearby, this mountain spring pooled into a lake inhabited by the same kinds of crocodiles and fish found in Egypt. From the lake, the waters of the Nile flowed deep underground emerging south of the Atlas Mountains; here it formed another lake which contained the same creatures. Juba thought the river buried itself again coming forth only when it reached the Niger River. From there it flowed east underground to Ethiopia where it, now called Astapus raced past Meroe and Elephantine and into Egypt. Juba had taken the accounts of merchants, soldiers, ancient colonizers, and explorers and stitched together a fascinating but ultimately erroneous theory of riverine geography. Undoubtedly he knew of the rivers Nile, Niger, Senegal, and possibly the underground water courses of the trans-Saharan region. He sought vainly to connect the abundant forests, teeming savannahs, and bountiful rivers in Africa to a single mother source.

Juba also wrote a geography of Arabia. Pliny, in *Historica Naturalis*, reserves high praise for this work and notes that Juba's text was his chief reference source for his description of Arabia. Juba dedicated this geography to the grandson of Emperor Augustus, a young man named Gaius Caesar, who later became the emperor Caligula.

Juba is also recognized as the discoverer of the Canaries, a group of islands in the Atlantic Ocean off the Spanish coast. He planned and organized an exploration of the islands. His sailors brought back remarkably accurate information on the animals and plants of the Canaries or the "Fortunate Islands" as they were known then. In his report of the voyage Juba described the environment of six of the seven most fertile islands and gave names for them: Jumonia, Ombrios, Nivaria, Capraria, and Canaria (Grand Canary). Ninguaria or Snow Island is how he described Mt. Tenerife and the swirl of winds that topped its peak with frosty clouds.

Pliny reproduced Juba's sailing directions "...from the Purple Islands proceed 250 miles to W., then 375 miles to E." The location of the "Purple Islands" is unclear but they are probably some of the tiny islands near the Straits of Gibraltar. Some experts believe that Pliny's directions are a result of an error in translation.

Juba's party found the Canaries empty of human life. Nuts, palms, lizards, and goats were found. Large dogs were found on one island and in honor of that it was named Insula Canaria from the Latin word "Canis" which means dog. Two of these huge hounds were taken back to Juba.

Pliny lists Juba as the discoverer of some tiny islands off the coast of Mauretania where the king built a factory to process purple dye from shellfish. Pliny called the islands "Purpurariae." Purple was the color of rank and wealth throughout the ancient world. Purple was another name for the rank of the Roman emperor. The name came from the color of his dyed woolen robe. To be "raised to the purple" even today means to be awarded high rank.

Juba also showed himself to be a wise ruler. He sought to help his kingdom struggle with the heavy taxes it was forced to pay to Rome each year. Juba married twice; first to Cleopatra Selene, the daughter of Cleopatra and Mark Antony. His second wife was Glaphyra, the Daughter of the king of Cappadocia, an ancient region of Turkey.

Like Prince Henry the Navigator of Portugal, who came more than a thousand years after him, Juba's first love was of the sea and ships and the exploration of new frontiers. King Juba died in 25 A.D.

Leo Africanus

Traveller. Geographer. Chronicler of new lands. All of these names described a man who was a Moor born in Spain in 1494. He was originally named Al Hassan Ibn Mohammed al-Wazzani.

Around 1510, he became an envoy in the diplomatic service of Morocco. His family had settled there after returning from Spain. In 1510, Leo went on what became the first of many trips deep into Africa. From Fez, he journeyed in a caravan to the Empire of Songhay. Impressed and curious about the luxury and sophistication of Songhay, he returned again in 1513. By now he had established his basic research methods: minute observation, exacting recall, collection of notes, interviews with commoners and royalty. On this journey, Leo accompanied his uncle, a trader and envoy from Morocco. Two years of travel brought Leo into contact with fifteen African kingdoms or empires. He travelled across the Atlas Mountains through the Sahara to Timbuktu. From there he crossed Africa, ending his trek at Dongola in the Sudan.

Christian pirates seized Leo in 1518 as he was sailing the Mediterranean Sea. He stunned them with vivid descriptions of the places he visited, Armenia, Arabia, and Central Asia. They were so moved by his knowledge of various parts of the world and his overall erudition that they gave him as a present to Pope Leo X in Rome. This Leo was the tenth of thirteen holy men to bear the name. Two of them achieved sainthood. Pope Leo X presided over a religious empire on the verge of disintegration. Concerns about nepotism, corruption, secular involvement, and the selling of indulgences threatened and in fact did fracture catholicism. This also led to the rise of Martin Luther and the beginning of Protestantism.

Pope Leo, a member of the de'Medici family and a rich and well educated man, became immediately fond of the young African scholar. The Pope soon freed him, granted him a stipend, and bestowed upon him his own name. When Leo was captured by the pirates one of the few things remaining in his possession was a draft manuscript in Arabic of his great work *The History and Description of Africa and the Notable Things Therein Contained*. Leo rewrote the entire work in Italian and published it in 1526. Dr. Benjamin Quarles has written that "Leo's work gave to his contemporaries and to the world the first detailed account of the wide regions that he had traversed." In 1600, John Pory, an associate of the English geographer and historian Richard Hakluyt, published an English version. What follows is Pory's English translation edited by Robert Brown. Leo Africanus describes Djenne (Ghinea), Melle and Tombuto (Timbuktu).

A DESCRIPTION OF THE KINGDOME OF GHINEA

This kingdom called by the merchants of our nation Gheneoa, by the natural inhabitants thereof Genni, and by the Portugals and other people of Europe, Ghinea, standeth in the midst between Gualata on the north, Tombuto on the east, and the kingdome of Meli on the south. In length it containeth almost five hundred miles, and extendeth two hundred and fiftie miles along the river of Niger, and bordereth upon the Ocean sea in the same place, where Niger falleth into the saide sea. This place exceedingly aboundeth with barlie, rice, cattell, fishes, and cotton: and their cotton they sell unto the merchants of Barbarie, for cloth of Europe, for brazen vessels, for armour, and other such commodities. Their coine is of gold without any stampe or inscription at all: they have certaine iron-money also, which they use about matters of small value, some pieces whereof weigh a pound, some halfe a pound, and some one quarter of a pound. In all this kingdome there is not fruite to be found but onely dates, which are brought hither either out of Gualata or Numidia. Heere is neither towne nor castle, but a certaine great village onely, wherein the prince of Ghinea, together with his priestes, doctors, merchants, and all the principle men of the region inhabite. The walles of their houses are built of chalke, and the roofes are covered with strawe: the inhabitants are clad in blacke or blew cotton, wherewith they cover their heads also: but the priests and doctors of their law go apparelled in white cotton. This region during the three moneths of Iulie, August and September, is yeerely environed with the overflowings of Niger in manner of an Island; all which time the merchants of Tombuto conveigh their merchandize hither in certaine Canoas or narrow boats made of one tree, which they rowe all the day long, but at night they binde them to the shore, and lodge themselves upon the lande.

OF THE KINGDOME OF MELLI

This region extending it selfe almost three hundred miles along the side of a river which falleth into Niger, bordereth northward upon the region last described, southward upon certaine deserts and drie mountaines, westward upon huge woods and forrests stretching to the Ocean sea shore, and eastward upon the territorie of Gago. In this kingdome there is a large and ample village containing to the number of sixe thousand or more families, and called Melli, whereof the whole kingdome is so named. And here the king hath his place of residence. The region it selfe yeeldeth great abundance of corne, flesh, and cotton. Heere are many artificers and merchants in all places: and yet the king honourably entertaineth all strangers. The inhabitants are rich, and have plentie of wares. Heere are great store of temples, priests, and professours, which professours read their lectures onely in the temples, bicause they have no colleges at all. The people of this region excell all other Negros in witte, civilitie, and industry; and were the first that embraced the law of Mahumet.

OF THE KINGDOME OF TOMBUTO

This name was in our times (as some thinke) imposed upon this kingdome from the name of certain towne so called, which (they say) king *Mense Suleiman* founded in the yeere of the Hegeira 610, and it is situate within twelve miles of a certaine branch of Niger, all the houses whereof are now changed into cottages built of chalke, and covered with thatch. Howbeit there is a most stately temple to be seene, the wals whereof are made of stone and lime; and a princely palace also built by a most excellent workeman of Granada. Here are many shops of artificers, and merchants, and especially of such as weave linnen and cotton cloth. And hither do the Barbarie-maid-servants go with their faces covered, and sell all necessarie victuals. The inhabitants, & especially strangers there residing, are exceeding rich, insomuch, that the king that now is [1526], married both his daughters unto two rich merchants. Here are many wels, containing most sweete water; and so often as the river Niger, overfloweth, they conveigh the water thereof by certaine sluces into the towns. Corne, cattle, milke, and butter this region yeeldeth in great abundance: but salt is very scare heere; for it is bought hither by land from Tegaza, which is five hundred miles distant. When I my selfe was here, I

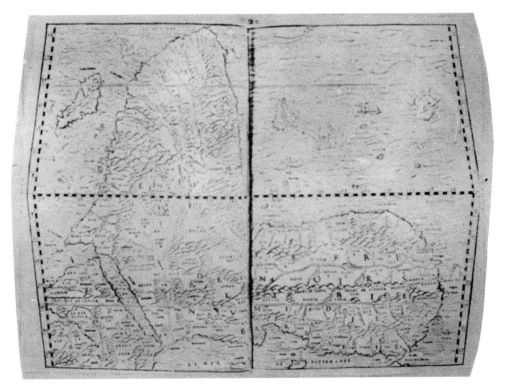

Figure 6

Map of Africa as it appeared in the 1556 edition of Leo Africanus' book, published in France.

saw one camels loade of salt sold for 80. ducates. The rich king of Tombuto hath many plates and scepters of gold, some whereof weigh 1300. pounds: and he keepes a magnificent and well furnished court. When he travelleth any whither he rideth upon a camell, which is lead by some of his noblemen; and so he doth likewise when hee goeth to warfar, and all his souldiers ride upon horses.

By the time of Pory's translation, Leo Africanus had been dead for eight years. His work survives and has been continuously used by scholars from the time of its original publication until today.

Figure 7
Martin R. Delany

Martin R. Delany and Robert Campbell

Martin Robinson Delany and Robert Campbell were the first African Americans to conduct their own private exploration in Africa.

Both men came from different backgrounds, were of different ages, and achieved different destinies. Their uniting beliefs were in Pan-Africanism, in Black nationalism, and in a return to an African homeland for the millions of descendants of African slaves forcibly brought to labor in the Americas by European colonizers.

Martin Delany was born in 1812 in what is now Charleston, West Virginia. He was the son of Samuel Delany, a slave, and Pati (Peace) Delany a free black woman. His grandparents were native Africans. One grandfather was a Mandingo prince. Another was the chief of a Golah village.

Delany was held spellbound by stories of Africa told to him by his maternal grandmother Graci Peace. She told him about mighty warriors, proud queens and African cultures equal to any in the world. She told him in almost mystical tones about her husband Shango. The stories heard in his youth fortified and galvanized Delany. They also instilled in him a great desire to return to the land of his ancestors.

Delany received his early education in Chambersburg, Pennsylvania. At the age of nineteen, he travelled to Pittsburgh, furthered his education, and began the study of medicine. Five years after arriving in Pittsburgh, his intellect and energy had pushed him into the leading rank of the city's black community. About this time he also began to participate in the local Underground Railroad, the black convention movement, and to lecture publicly against slavery. Between 1843 and 1864 he married and had seven children that lived through infancy. Each child was named after a famous black person. His sons were named Charles Lenox Redmond, Alexander Dumas, Faustin Soulouque, Saint Cyprian, Toussaint L'Overture, and Ramses Placido. His daughter was named Ethiopia Halle Delany.

Delany published and edited *The Mystery*, the first black newspaper west of the Allegheny Mountains and served as co-editor with Frederick Douglass of the *North Star*. In November 1850 he spent a semester studying medicine at Harvard but was dismissed because of protests by white students in 1851. He was deeply affected by the passage of the Fugitive Slave Act in 1850 which essentially brought the power of the federal government into the efforts by slaveholders to recover their runaway slaves from free states or territories and return them to slavery.

Secluded in a New York boarding house, Delany wrote *The Condition, Elevation, Emigration, and Destiny of the Colored People of the United States, Politically Considered*. Historians consider this the first full length discussion of black nationalism. Published in 1852, the work's discussion of large scale black emigration from the United States ignited widespread debate in the black community. In the appendix to the book, Delany suggested an "expedition to the Eastern Coast of Africa" to determine the area's suitability for settlement.

The book also led directly to the organization of a National Emigration Convention that met in Cleveland in 1854. At this meeting a National Board of Commissioners was established, and led by Delany, it evaluated various locations in the West Indies, Central and

A Pilgrimage to My Motherland.

AN

ACCOUNT OF A JOURNEY

AMONG

THE EGBAS AND YORUBAS OF CENTRAL AFRICA,

In 1859-60.

BY

ROBERT CAMPBELL,

One of the Commissioners of the Niger Valley Exploring Party; late in charge of the Scientific Department of the Institute for Colored Youth, Philadelphia; and Member of the International Statistical Congress, London.

New-York:

PUBLISHED BY THOMAS HAMILTON, 48 BEEKMAN ST.

PHILADELPHIA:

BY THE AUTHOR, 661 NORTH THIRTEENTH ST.

1861.

Figure 8

Robert Campbell and the title page of his book

South America, and finally Africa. In the spring of 1858, Delany was busy recruiting members of his exploring party and soliciting funds to cover expenses. Friends of Delany's in Philadelphia suggested Robert Campbell as a replacement for someone who could not go on the trip.

Robert Campbell was a young, fervent Pan Africanist and black nationalist. Born in Jamaica, in 1829, Campbell was the science teacher at the Institute for Colored Youth in Philadelphia. He had arrived in New York in 1853, after a career as a printer, teacher, and traveller in Central America. Outspoken and as strong willed as Delany, Campbell often sharply disagreed with him over methods but never over objectives.

Delany hoped that by signing treaties with local chiefs land would become available for a colony of black "persons to fill every vocation necessary to an intelligent and progressive community." The colony would support itself through cotton or other crops, demonstrate the capability of blacks for intelligent self-rule, and limit European expansion in Africa. At the meeting of the third Emigration Convention in August 1858, Delany listed the men who were to take part in his projected "Topographical, Geological, and Geographical examination of the valley of the River Niger." Delany, the leader, selected Robert Campbell, naturalist; Robert Douglass, artist; Dr. Amos Aray, surgeon; and James W. Purnell, secretary and commercial reporter. Douglass, Aray and Purnell dropped out of the project.

Delany's plans were also nearly wrecked by anti-emigrationist forces at the convention. Many black leaders outside the convention openly criticized aspects of Delany's mission or attempted to begin rival ventures by joining with rich whites. Delany refused to accept help from whites. By contrast, Campbell felt he had to get to Africa no matter who paid. His resolve was firm. His commitment to the colony secure.

Campbell arrived in England in May 1859 where he solicited money, obtained maps from the Royal Geographical Society, and met with English abolitionists and cotton industry representatives.

Both Delany and Campbell arrived in Lagos, in what is now Nigeria in July, 1859 after stopovers in Liberia. Campbell went ahead to Abeokuta eager to begin. With the help of Samuel Adjai Crowther, a well-known black minister and head of an influential family, Delany and Campbell were drawn to Nigeria because of several favorable reports on the fertility of the land.

Crowther knew the area well and believed Abeokuta an excellent base of operations. He was also an experienced explorer. He had accompanied J.F. Schon on a missionary survey of the area in 1841. Crowther also travelled with the Scottish scientist W.B. Baikie on two expeditions into the Niger Delta.

Campbell learned that one of the local rulers, the Alake of Abeokuta, wanted to offer land. Abeokuta, founded in 1830, was a prosperous trading town on the Ogun River not far from the coast. Campbell also learned that Rev. Henry Townsend, an English missionary who was a friend of the Alake, had advised against helping them.

Delany joined Campbell in Abeokuta in November. The day after Christmas, 1859, Delany and Campbell signed a treaty with the Alake permitting African Americans to settle around Abeokuta.

In Campbell's book, *A Pilgrimage to My Motherland*, published in 1861, Campbell describes the Alake as a "good-natured fat old gentleman, giving himself only so much concern about public affairs as to secure the good will of his.... chiefs." The Alake had "great energy and decision of character."

Campbell was deeply touched at his meeting with the elderly Chief Atambala or Age'. As usual by now the light-skinned Campbell mentioned that he was of African descent. "On learning this, he took hold of my hand and shook it heartily; and drawing me toward him, he threw his arms about my neck and pressed me with warmth." Delany and Campbell were warmly received by the Africans from the beginning. In Liberia and Nigeria they addressed enthusiastic crowds. They were treated, Campbell observed, as long lost relatives.

In mid-January, Delany and Campbell began their explorations in southwestern Nigeria. They travelled through Egbaland and Yorubaland reaching Ikaye, Oyo, Ogbomishaw, and Ilorin. A border dispute between ethnic groups and a desire to explore a larger area prompted Delany and Campbell to split up. Campbell headed farther west through Ischin Awaye, Bioloranpellu and Berecada. Delany worked his way east and south past Iwo and Ibadan. They crossed the swelling rivers and productive lowlands of the south which rose to a series of hills and plateaus in the center of the country.

Everything the two men saw, the verdant landscape and the friendly people, strengthened their resolve to build homes, and establish farms and businesses in Nigeria. The heart of their colony would be the city of Abeokuta.

While Delany and Campbell were up river, Townsend and his cronies attacked the legitimacy of the treaty. Townsend believed Africans unfit for self-government. He also objected to rumored plans to make Samuel Adjai Crowther an Anglican bishop for West Africa. Crowther responded to Townsend's charges.

Delany and Campbell returned to Abeokuta undaunted by the controversy. After nine months in West Africa, they returned to the United States after stopping in England. While there, Delany and Campbell won praise for their explorations. Delany spoke before the Royal Geographical Society and the International Statistical Congress which both men joined.

In the United States, Delany and Campbell, dressed in traditional Nigerian robes, mesmerized audiences with stories of their travels and busily signed on potential settlers for Africa. In 1861, Delany wrote the major account of the trip, *Official Report of the Niger Valley Exploring Party*. In his 1874 book, *The Rising Son*, William Wells Brown, a black author and journalist, noted that Delany did not visit Nigeria "with his eyes shut. His observations and suggestions about the climate, soil, diseases and natural productions of Africa are interesting and give evidence the doctor was in earnest. The published report of which he is the author will repay a perusal." Delany and Campbell continued to travel, make presentations, and recruit pioneers even as most African Americans and the rest of the nation turned its attention to the Civil War.

Delany soon used his formidable energies to enlist black men to fight in the Union Army. In February 1865, he received a commission as the first black major in the United States Army. After the war, Delany became involved in southern politics, wrote *Principia of Ethnology: The Origin of Races and Color*, in which he attempted to decipher hieroglyphics, discuss classical African civilizations, and explain the properties of melanin (he called it pigmentum nigrum). He also worked with the Liberian Exodus Joint Stock Exchange Company, a group carrying African Americans to Liberia. Delany died in 1885.

Campbell indicated his state of mind at the end of the preface to his book: "After what is written in the context, if I am still asked what I think of Africa for a colored man to live and do well in, I simply answer, that with as good prospects in America as colored men generally, I have determined, with my wife and children, to go to Africa to live, leaving the inquirer to interpret the reply for himself."

Campbell returned to Lagos in 1862. He founded and edited the *Anglo-African Weekly*. Pan-Africanist in theme, its message was far too dangerous for British colonial and missionary interests. The paper soon ceased operations. But Campbell and his family remained in Africa.

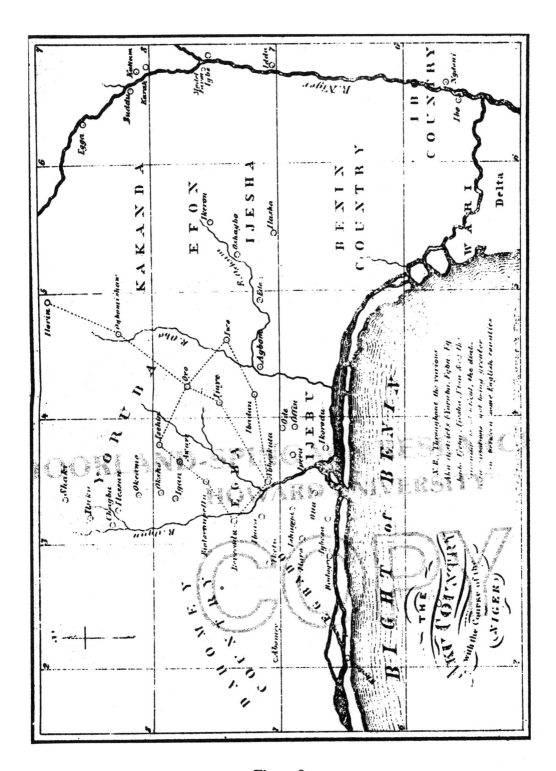

Figure 9

A map of Delany and Campbell's expedition in Nigeria (from Campbell's book)

Benjamin J. K. Anderson

Benjamin Anderson led expeditions across Liberia in 1868 and 1874, and is believed to have gone as far east as the border with Guinea.

Today, Liberia, a nation in West Africa, occupies 38,250 square miles, a territory only slightly smaller than the state of Pennsylvania. The present size of the country and the security of its current borders would never have been respected by the international community without explorers such as Benjamin Anderson.

Liberia was founded in 1822 by African Americans with the help of the American Colonization Society, a group of whites seeking to settle emancipated black Americans in Africa. In 1847 the black settlers ended their association with the colonization society and formally declared themselves the independent Republic of Liberia. The name is based on the Latin word "liber" which means free.

The nation found itself born into a hostile environment. Slave dealing was widespread. European slave ships ignored Liberian sovereignty. Profits from the selling of camwood, ivory, coffee, and palm oil desperately needed by the Liberian territory disappeared into the pockets of greedy traders and local chiefs willing to ignore the government. Most troubling to the future of the republic was the appropriation of large amounts of Liberian territory by neighboring European colonies. The year after independence was declared, France occupied what is now Guinea and began moving its border west into Liberia. The British from Sierra Leone and the French from their protectorate on the Ivory Coast also greedily eyed Liberia.

Liberia desperately needed room to grow. In the first twenty years of the country's independence, six thousand black Americans, fed up with racism and discrimination, emigrated to Liberia. With the help of the indigenous Africans of the coast and interior these settlers could expand agricultural production, establish factories, and develop commerce.

In 1868, Benjamin Anderson, "a young man educated in Liberia, of pure negro blood" volunteered to lead an expedition to the eastern frontier. His goal was the trade center of Musahdu, in an area controlled by the Mandingos. Ten years earlier, President Benson dispatched two Liberians, Seymour and Ash to explore the same territory. The Royal Geographical Society in England, published an account of their expedition. It was too soon after independence for the chronically cash-short country to follow up on the entire report.

Anderson was about thirty-four years old and living the comfortable life of a bureaucrat in Monrovia, the Liberian capital. He served in President Warner's cabinet as Secretary of the Treasury. He shook off the trappings of urban life, collected his supplies and made his way east. Two hundred miles separated him from his destination.

From the low flat coastline indented by a series of rivers, Liberia rises to rolling plains and squat mountains in the northeast. The climate in the back country ranges from hot, humid days and nights through the rain forest to cool, even cold nights in the high country. Anderson struggled through the rough terrain, committing all the mistakes of a novice on the trail. Equipment was lost or stolen. His guides deserted him. Anderson kept going on. It was here that a local African chief's observation of Anderson's determined character

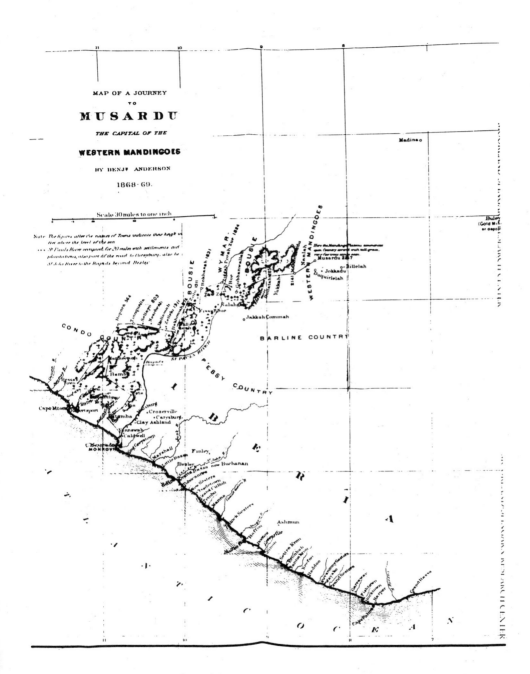

Figure 10

Benjamin Anderson's map of his travels

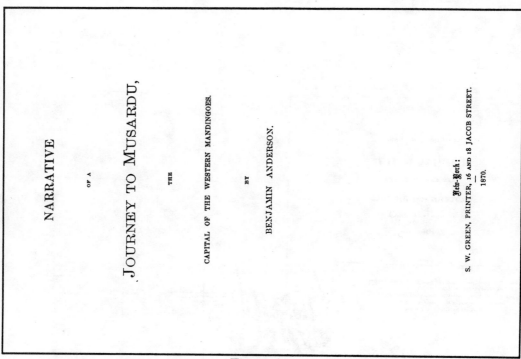

Figure 11

Anderson's description of his first journey

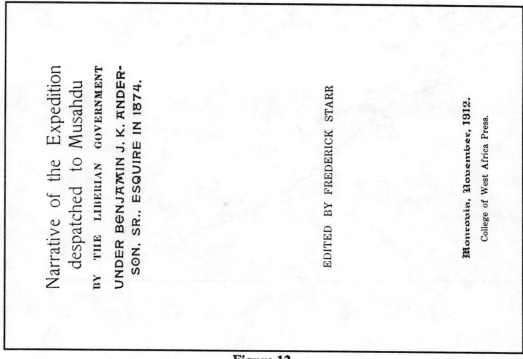

Figure 12

Anderson's account of his second expedition was not formally
published until more than a decade after it took place.

proved itself on the mark. He told one of Anderson's men, "Your daddy has got the heart of an elephant." As Anderson reached the plains, he saw fields full of produce, and large walled cities. Such a place was Musahdu. The city was ruled by a Muslim king strong enough to put a cavalry of fifteen hundred into the field. Anderson was well received in Musahdu, fed and entertained.

Anderson toured the surrounding cities noting the wealth of the inhabitants, their military capabilities, and the hospitality extended to him by nearly everyone. Word of mouth carried news of his arrivals far ahead of him. Local monarchs asked him about the peoples of the coast whom they assumed were mostly Christians and Jews. Most of the rulers expressed their desire for increased trade and their curiosity about the government in Monrovia and its intentions.

Anderson made precise geographical sightings, noted carefully the locations of the towns, and drew maps of his line of march. Anderson evidently crossed into Guinea believing it still was rightfully part of Liberia. French colonial administrators disputed Anderson's claims. Recent research seems to bear out the accuracy of Anderson's expedition. An 1894 French map of the area even appears to have relied on Anderson's travels.

In 1870 in New York City, Anderson published a description of his trip. The title of the book is *Narrative of a Journey to Musardu, the Capital of the Western Mandingoes.*

An appendix to the account of Anderson's trip is also interesting. The appendix contains a copy of an Arabic manuscript written by Mohammed Barta, a young man at the court of the king. The English translation of the manuscript was written by Edward Wilmot Blyden, the famous West Indian scholar who settled in Liberia.

The manuscript provides a history of the area around Musahdu, the wars between the rulers of the various towns, some of which were Muslim while other towns were led by rulers following traditional African religion. Anderson's arrival in Musahdu is also mentioned. The manuscript closes with a request for assistance from the government in Monrovia including missionaries and teachers.

In 1874, the Liberian government authorized Anderson to make a second exploration of the area.

Anderson wrote a book about his second journey. It was entitled *Narrative of the Expedition Dispatched to Musahdu by the Liberian Government.* The Liberian government never published this book. Except for a serialization in *The Observer*, a Monrovia newspaper, no account of Anderson's second trip appeared until 1912 when five hundred copies were published in Monrovia by the College of West Africa Press.

Tippu Tip

His real name was Hamed bin Muhammad bin Juna al-Marjebi. His nickname was Tippu Tip (or Tippu Tib); it meant "whistling bullets." Everywhere that he went it was said "the bullets whistled." Tippu Tip's relentless search for slaves, gold, and ivory marked him as the greatest single slaver in the history of East Africa. To accomplish this, he explored thousands of square miles of east African territory leaving death and massive dislocation of cultures in his wake. His slaving raids helped weaken eastern Africa and allow the eventual domination of the area by the European colonial powers. He realized too late what he had done. When he fought back he was finally betrayed by one of his lieutenants.

In *The Race to Fashoda*, David Levering Lewis describes Tippu Tip as "The son of a Zanzibar Arab father and an unmixed African slave, master of East Africa from the Tanganyika Coast to where the swift Lualaba halfway runs its course to the Congo."

Tippu Tip was born on the island of Zanzibar around 1850. His father was a trader on the African mainland and often took his son along. His imagination fired by the stories he heard around safari campfires, Tippu Tip decided to lead his own caravan on a trading mission. After some initial setbacks, he and his men were underway. In the territory of King Nsana, whom Livingstone had called the "Napoleon of Africa," Tippu Tip waged a four-day battle and then defeated the King. When King Nsana's subjects learned he was defeated many of them rose in rebellion. Tippu Tip and the rest of the Arab slavers promoted and profited from ethnic rivalries and disputes.

John A. Hunter and Daniel P. Mannix's *Tales of the African Frontier* describe Tippu Tip's methods as quoted in *The Great Explorers* by Helen Wright and Samuel Rappaport:

> The formula was now complete. From then on, Tippu Tib applied it with almost monotonous regularity. The Arabs would move into a village and offer to buy ivory. As all the native tribes were hostile to each other, jealous neighbors would sooner or later attack the village. Then the Arabs would support their friends. The Arab guns always decided the issue and the winning tribe, confident that the victory was due solely to their own tribal courage and ability, would start on a career of conquest. Eventually they would turn on the Arabs. Then the Arabs would form a confederation against them and soon they would go the same path as their victims. In this way, the power of Tippu Tib continued to grow and a constant stream of ivory and slaves flowed out of Central Africa to Zanzibar.

By the 1870s, Tippu Tip had expanded his operations hundreds of miles into the interior. While some historians have painted Tippu Tip as a peaceful man who only engaged reluctantly in battle, eyewitnesses to his cruelty leave no doubt as to Tippu Tip's regard for the Africans. *The Exploration Diaries of H.M. Stanley* for November 7, 1876 records these events:

> Halt at Mpotira [downstream from Nyangwe], to allow a winding caravan under our escort to come up with hundreds of sheep and goats which they are taking to Tata for trade. A sheep is said to purchase one

Figure 13
Tippu Tip

[tusk of] ivory, 12 slaves purchase an ivory. In Ujiji 6 slaves purchase an ivory.

"Slaves cost nothing," said Hamed bin Mohammed, "they only require to be gathered." And that is the work of Muini Dugumbi and Mtagamoyo [Tippu Tip's companions].

These half-castes of Nyangwe have no cloth or beads or wares of merchandise. They obtain their ivory by robbing... They attack the simple peoples of Nyangwe right and left, 12 or 15 slaves then caught are sold for 35 pounds (16 kilos) of ivory. Muini Dugumbi has one hundred to one hundred and twenty women. Mtagamoyo has 60...

Tippu Tip's slaving raids made him a wealthy man. He also was a fervent Muslim. In his business dealings he performed every courtesy. In his religion he was exemplary. Polite to guests, hospitable to strangers, Tippu Tip saw the slave trade as a business. He effectively controlled the access routes into the interior. None of the European explorers could pass through his dominions without his permission. From him they had to seek porters for their supplies and guides for their destinations. And he never refused them. In volume one of *World's Great Men of Color*, J.A. Rogers quotes portions of an interview between Tippu Tip and Alfred Swann, a British colonial official:

If I had wished to stop him [Stanley], I should not have played with the matter by sending 400 men instead of 600, as per contract. I should have killed him long ago. I do not simply hinder, I destroy. If I assist, it is at all costs.

Who helped Cameron, Speke, Livingstone? Who sent Glerrup from the Congo to Sweden? Who saved your life and those of all your party?

Without my help he [Stanley] could never have gone down the Congo, and no sooner did he reach Europe than he claimed all my territory...

Tell Europe Stanley lies, and tell them also, if they love justice as you say, to compensate me for stealing my country.

Tippu Tip saw the increasing presence of Europeans as a threat to Arab control of the slave, gold, and ivory trades. He became further alarmed when he learned the German government claimed the East African territory of Tanganyika and that the German fleet had sailed into the harbor of Zanzibar, his offshore island headquarters. His nemesis, Stanley arrived with a message from King Leopold of Belgium offering to name Tippu Tip governor of the Congo, a region he already controlled!

By 1890 Tippu Tip had decided to leave the mainland and turn the slaving business over to his son, Sefu. Before he left his son they agreed on an all out attack to drive the European out of Central Africa. In 1892, Sefu's men attacked Belgian positions along the Lualaba River. Several early successes were achieved. Ngongo Leteta, one of Tippu Tip's deputies, suddenly switched sides adding nearly 10,000 men to the Belgian force. Sefu was soon killed in battle. Incredibly, the Belgians soon doublecrossed and executed Ngongo Leteta. The revolt was over. The Arab slave empire had been crushed. Europe divided Tippu Tip's domain. Belgium got the Congo. Germany and Great Britain received East Africa.

Tippu Tip died in 1905.

Swann's interview also contained this remarkable exchange with Tippu Tip. When Swann commented on the cruelty of the Arab slaver, Tippu Tip replied:

"Is that so?" exclaimed Tippu Tib. "How did you get India?"

"We fought for it."

"Then what you fight for and win belongs to you by right of conquest?"

"Yes, that is European law."

"So it is with us Arabs. I came here a young man, fought these natives and subdued them, losing both friends and treasure in the struggle. Is it not therefore mine by both your law and ours?

"It is only yours as long as you govern and use it properly."

"Who is to be my judge?"

"Europe!"

"Ah!" said the Arab, smiling grimly. "Now you speak the truth. Do not let us talk of justice. People are only just when it pays. The white man is stronger than I am. They will eat up my possessions as I ate those of the pagans, and..."

He paused and then went on fiercely: "Finally someone will eat up yours! The day is not as far off as you think. I see the clouds gathering in the sky. I hear the thunder!"

Paul Belloni Du Chaillu

"I travelled-always on foot, and unaccompanied by other white men-about 8,000 miles. I shot, stuffed and brought home over 2,000 birds, of which more than 60 are new species, and I killed upwards of 1,000 quad-ruped, of which 200 were stuffed and brought home, with more than 80 hitherto unknown to science. I suffered fifty attacks of the African fever, taking, to cure myself, more than fourteen ounces of quinine. Of famine, long-continued exposures to the heavy tropical rains, and attacks of fero-cious ants and venomous flies, it is not worth while to speak."

Paul Belloni Du Chaillu was one of the greatest men in the history of African explora-tion. Explorer, anthropologist, and traveller, Du Chaillu is recognized as the first to bring back tangible evidence of the gorilla. From the time of Hanno's voyage about 500 B.C. and his reported encounter with hairy men and women whom his "interpreters called gorillas," the existence of such creatures was the subject of scientific speculation. Stories of cunning, cruel, giant "men of the woods" kidnapping African girls for unspeakable purposes or attacking Africans for no apparent reasons could not be verified. In 1847, an American missionary sent the skull of a Gabon gorilla, an anthropoid ape to a Boston naturalist and Hanno's story began to be taken more seriously.

It remained for Du Chaillu to bring back enough gorilla specimens to end scientific debate and firmly place the gorilla in its proper scientific category. Du Chaillu grew up travelling with his father, a French trader in West Africa. From his father's "factory or depot" in Gabon, the young man ventured to the local missionary schools playing with and learning from the African children and adults living or working in those places. He found himself increasingly drawn to African life. The culture and environment fascinated him. Du Chaillu learned the African ways well. Not only did he explore only with Africans, unlike Stanley or several other explorers, he never killed an African.

In 1852, or 1853, he travelled to the United States. His knowledge of Africa interested members of the scientific community. In 1855, the Academy of Natural Sciences, in Philadelphia backed his requests to lead an expedition into the interior of Africa to collect specimens of animal life. The following year he landed on the Gabon coast. Du Chaillu began a three year trek into Africa, that took him 320 miles inland and 250 miles north and south. Du Chaillu ranged over a wide area of what is now the Gabonese Republic. He endured its tropical heat and shot or captured animals from the country's hilly midlands to its savannahs in its eastern region.

Back in the United States in 1859, Du Chaillu published two years later *Explorations and Adventures in Equatorial Africa; with Accounts of the manners and customs of the people, and of the Chase of the Gorilla, Crocodile, Leopard, Elephant, Hippopotamus, and other animals. By Paul B. Duchaillu, with Map and Illustrations.*

Du Chaillu's first book received mixed reviews. As a literary work, he was a gifted natural storyteller. As a work of science, many of his contemporaries sneered at his prose and considered his observations exaggerated. Later investigations by others proved much of Du Chaillu's writings accurate. From *Explorations and Adventures in Equatorial Africa...*, here is Du Chaillu's first meeting with a gorilla:

Figure 14
Paul Belloni DuChaillu

The underbrush swayed rapidly just ahead, and presently before us stood an immense male gorilla. He had gone through the jungle on his all-fours, but when he saw our party he erected himself, and looked us boldly in the face. He stood about a dozen yards from us, and was a sight I think I shall never forget. Nearly six feet high (he proved four inches shorter,) with immense body, huge chest, and great muscular arms, with fiercely glaring, large, deep-gray eyes, and a hellish expression of face, which seemed to me like some nightmare vision; thus stood before us the king of the African forest. He was not afraid of us. He stood there and beat his breast with his huge fists, till it resounded like an immense bass-drum, which is their mode of offering defiance, meantime giving vent to roar after roar. The roar of the gorilla is the most singular and awful noise heard in these African woods. It begins with a sharp bark like an angry dog, then glides into a deep bass roll which literally and closely resembles the roll of distant thunder along the sky, for which I have been sometimes tempted to take it when I did not see the animal. So deep is it that it seems to proceed less from the mouth and throat than from the deep chest and vast paunch. His eyes began to flash deeper fire as we stood motionless on the defensive, and the crest of short hair which stands on his forehead began to twitch rapidly up and down, while his powerful fangs were shown as he again sent forth a thunderous roar. And now truly he reminded me of nothing but some hellish dream-creature; a being of that hideous order, half-man, half-beast, which we find pictured by old artists in some representations of the infernal regions. He advanced a few steps, then stopped to utter that hideous roar again, advanced again, and finally stopped when at a distance of about six yards from us. And here, just as he began another of his roars, beating his breast in rage, we fired and killed him. With a groan which had something terribly human in it, and yet was full of brutishness, he fell foreward on his face. The body shook convulsively for a few minutes, the limbs moved about in a struggling way, and then all was quiet-death had done its work, and I had leisure to examine the huge body. It proved to be five feet eight inches high, and the muscular development of the arms and breast showed what immense strength he had possessed.

In *Stories of the Gorilla Country*, written a short time later, DuChaillu describes the death of one of the largest snakes he had ever seen:

After resting a little while we continued our course till we reached the top of a very high mountain, whence I could see all the country round. I was sitting under a very large tree, when suddenly looking up, I saw an immense serpent coiled upon the branch of a tree just above me. I rushed out, and taking good aim with my gun, I shot my black friend in the head. He let go his hold, tumbled down with great force, and after writhing convulsively for a time, he lay before me dead. He measured thirteen feet in length, and his ugly fangs proved that he was venomous. My men cut off the head of the snake, and divided the body into as many parts as their

EXPLORATIONS & ADVENTURES

IN

EQUATORIAL AFRICA;

WITH ACCOUNTS OF THE MANNERS AND CUSTOMS OF THE PEOPLE, AND OF THE CHACE
OF THE *GORILLA*, CROCODILE, LEOPARD, ELEPHANT, HIPPOPOTAMUS,
AND OTHER ANIMALS.

By PAUL B. DU CHAILLU.

Ncheri—a diminutive Gazelle.

With Map and Illustrations.

LONDON:

JOHN MURRAY, ALBEMARLE STREET.

1861.

The right of Translation is reserved.

Figure 15

Figure 16

Female gorilla and young

Figure 17

Killing the snake — Central Africa

were people. Then they lighted a fire, and roasted and ate it on the spot. They offered me a piece, but though I was very hungry, I declined. When the snake was eaten, I was the only individual in the company that had an empty stomach.

Du Chaillu led another expedition into the same area in 1863 and confirmed the existence of groups of small Africans called by Europeans "pygmies" after the tiny peoples of Greek myth. From that two year exploration, Du Chaillu wrote *A Journey to Ashango-land and Further Penetration into Equatorial Africa.*

The maps of *A Journey to Ashango-land...* were widely hailed for their "unique value," according to the 1910 *Encyclopedia Britannica.* Du Chaillu settled in America basking in the light his fame provided but keeping to himself a secret that could bring his world to ruin.

When asked for biographical details Du Chaillu was evasive. The precise year of his birth is not agreed upon. It may be 1835 or 1837. His birthplace is listed as either Paris or New Orleans. Although recent Du Chaillu biographers, Vaucaire and Casada believe France to be his birthplace both admit to encountering the "clouded" circumstances of his birth.

In Volume one of *World's Great Men of Color,* J.A. Rogers uncovered Du Chaillu's closely guarded secret. Du Chaillu had been "born on the island of Reunion off the east coast of Africa of a French father and a mulatto mother." Rogers described Du Chaillu's predicament:

> In America, realizing that it would be fatal should his true ancestry be known, he evaded mention of the place of his birth, leaving the inquisitive to make their own guesses. Fortunately for him, though his skin was dark and was burned even darker by the African sun and his face was Negroid, his hair was straight. He was further helped by his foreign accent, and as he spoke French, it was generally said he was from New Orleans.

Du Chaillu wrote a series of African adventure books for children and lectured in the United States and Europe. One of his last American lectures was before the National Geographic Society. He wrote two books on the origins of the English people (See chapter four of this book). While travelling in Russia, he fell ill. He died in St. Petersburg in 1903.

George Washington Ellis

George Washington Ellis' eight years as an explorer was an extension of the valuable diplomatic work he performed while Secretary of the U.S. Legation in the Republic of Liberia.

Ellis arrived in Monrovia, the capital of Liberia in 1902. Born in 1875 in Missouri, Ellis practiced law in Kansas, studied at the Gunton Institute of Economics and Sociology in New York City, and in 1899 moved to Washington, D.C. to work at the Department of the Interior and study at Howard University. Ellis' voracious intellect covered an incredibly diverse range of topics including economics, literature, philosophy, history, psychology, languages, and African affairs.

It was Ellis' fascination with African history and culture that led him to accept the position in Liberia for which he had been initially recommended by President Theodore Roosevelt.

Liberia in the early 1900's faced problems similar to those which had inspired the explorations of Benjamin Anderson a few decades earlier. Liberia was still too poor to begin anything except the most modest internal improvements, slaving had been largely eliminated, but neighboring colonies established by European governments had become even more blatant in their attempts to swallow Liberian territory. The United States which served as a model for Liberia's government, constitution, currency, and law, provided no foreign aid. The United States did assure the government in Monrovia that it would assist the country in maintaining the sanctity of its borders.

The headquarters duties of the legation secretary were not burdensome. Ellis found that his true tasks were to observe, record, and collect information about the indigenous African peoples of Liberia, the Afro-Liberians as they are known today. Ellis was also to report on attempts by Britain and France to annex Liberian territory and convince the Liberian government of the United States' special historical and political if not financial interest in Liberia.

Ellis' trips brought him firsthand knowledge of the cultures and peoples of the various ethnic groups of the interior. A meticulous researcher, Ellis brought all his intellectual power to bear on the fascinating people and events he saw as he explored the country up river. He collected statues, weapons, cloths and data on rituals, symbology and religions, and became fluent in several of the local languages. He seems to have been aware of the expeditions of Benjamin Anderson and was convinced that in order for Liberia to survive and prosper external foreign influences had to be eliminated.

Ellis' reports to State Department headquarters in Washington, D.C. describe the difficulties faced by new black emigrants to Liberia, the social caste system erected by Americo-Liberians (the descendants of the original black American colonists) against Afro-Liberians, ethnic conflicts, and boundary negotiations between Britain, France, and Liberia. Detailed, perceptive, scholarly, Ellis' accounts guided U.S. policy toward Liberia during the first decade of the twentieth century.

Ellis presented a paper entitled *International Law As a Factor in Social Progress* to the Liberian National Bar Association in 1908.

Nearly constant exposure to heat, insects, and fever weakened Ellis' health substantial-

George Washington Ellis

NEGRO CULTURE IN WEST AFRICA

A SOCIAL STUDY OF THE NEGRO GROUP OF VAI-SPEAKING PEOPLE
WITH ITS OWN INVENTED ALPHABET AND WRITTEN LAN-
GUAGE SHOWN IN TWO CHARTS AND SIX ENGRAVINGS
OF VAI SCRIPT, TWENTY-SIX ILLUSTRATIONS OF
THEIR ARTS AND LIFE, FIFTY FOLKLORE STOR-
IES, ONE HUNDRED AND FOURTEEN PRO-
VERBS AND ONE MAP

By

GEORGE W. ELLIS, K.C., F.R.G.S.

For eight years Secretary of the United States Legation in
Liberia; author of "Liberia in the Political Psychology
of West Africa," "Islam as a Factor in West
African Culture," "Dynamic Factors in
the Liberian Situation," etc.

Introduction by
FREDERICK STARR, B.S., M.S., PH.D., Sc.D.
Professor and Curator of Anthropology in the University of Chicago

*To show the world—Africans helping in the work—that the African has a culture of his own—
to explain that culture, and assist him to develop it.—The African Journal and Mary H. Kingsley, p.1.
Edward Wilmot Blyden.*

NEW YORK
THE NEALE PUBLISHING COMPANY
1914

Leslie Lewis.

Figure 19

ly and undoubtedly was a factor in his decision to leave Liberia. The attitude of the State Department toward Ellis also was a source of disillusionment and anger. Despite his value to the State Department, Ellis never achieved a promotion higher than his original position. He resigned from the State Department in 1910.

Recognition did arrive from other quarters. Ellis was elected a fellow of the Royal Geographical Society of Great Britain. Shortly before leaving Liberia with his wife, Clavender Sherman Ellis, a Liberian, he was made a Knight Commander of the Order of African Redemption by the Liberian government.

Ellis settled in Chicago and established a famous and well-respected law practice. He also argued in front of the United States Supreme Court and served as an assistant corporation counsel for Chicago. He lectured widely on his travels in Liberia and dabbled in local politics.

From his home on Vernon Avenue in Chicago, Ellis produced a stream of writings on Africa. His best known work was *Negro Culture in West Africa*. This book examined the culture and history of the Vai people of Liberia and demonstrated that these Africans had produced their ''own invented alphabet and written language.'' Ellis included in the book six engravings and two charts of Vai script, twenty six illustrations on Vai life and arts, fifty folklore stories, one hundred fourteen Vai proverbs, and a map.

Prior to *Negro Culture in West Africa*, Ellis authored *Liberia in the Political Psychology of West Africa*, *Islam as a Factor in West African Culture*, and *Dynamic Factors in the Liberian Situation*. In 1917, Ellis wrote *The Leopard's Claw*, a novel of romance and suspense set in West Africa. He also wrote *Negro Achievements in Social Progress*.

Ellis contributed articles to the *Journal of International Relations*, and served as a contributing editor from 1910 to 1919. He continued an active schedule of public speaking. Ellis died in Chicago in 1919. In the March 1920 edition of *The Crisis*, a magazine published by the National Association for the Advancement of Colored People, his obituary began with the words:

> At the early age of forty four years, George Washington Ellis has finished his earthly career, but not without much work accomplished as an author, a lawyer, and a statesman.

CHAPTER 2

THE ANCIENT MARITIME HERITAGE OF AFRICA

Apart from the river and coastal trading commented upon by early visitors to Africa, there exists no image of the sailing or seagoing African in the minds of either the public or many historians.

Close scrutiny of available records, however, reveals that Africans have been innovative and daring sailors from history's earliest times. One of the oldest examples of this interest was discovered in 1988 in Egypt.

On a sandstone butte jutting 12 feet above the desert floor, archeologists found a black painting of a boat with oarsmen which they believe was made between 3200 B.C. and 2500 B.C. This places the rock painting or "petroglyph" at the dawn of pharaonic history during the reign of the first pharaoh, Narmer. This southern Egyptian king united Upper and Lower Egypt, the two lands, founding the first dynasty of Ancient Egypt and beginning a political system that lasted 3,000 years. Egypt, more correctly called by its African name, Kemet, was the world's first nation-state.

The late Dr. Michael Hoffman, then leader of the expedition that discovered the painting, called it "a mystery in progress. Some archeological finds you don't get excited about until you eventually recognize their significance. This one got us excited right away... It's telling us something we've never heard of before."

One early theory about the painting is that it was done by Nubian mercenaries camping by the butte who were working for Egyptians. Rock paintings are comparatively more common in Nubia and unknown in early Egypt. The site where the painting was discovered will be the subject of further research and the cause of much debate.

That ships and boats were important in Egyptian history is evident by the strong, even mystical attachment Egyptians felt to the Nile River. Flowing through the heart of their country, the Nile had helped unify the country by bringing together diverse groups of peoples for the common and necessary purpose of controlling its rising waters. They had overcome mutual suspicions and fear to band together to protect their fields, apportion and irrigate their lands. In the process, they laid the foundation for an empire.

The Nile, the world's longest river, is a nurturing ribbon of blue lying between amber-colored hills that warded off the desert and many invaders. To the ancient Egyptians, the Nile was lifeline, God, friend. Shrines to it were built along its banks. Hymns like this were sung to it: "Hail to you, O Nile! Sprung from earth, come to nourish Egypt!... Food provider, bounty maker, who creates all that is good."

The authors of Volume Two of the *UNESCO General History of Africa*, note that there were also practical considerations for the importance of the Nile to ancient Egypt. "The development of transport was one determining factor in the progress of the Pharaonic regime... For bulk transport over long distances, Egypt used its river and its canals; small craft and large boats were rapid and reliable. In addition, even at a very early date, sailing boats plied the Red Sea and the Mediterranean."

The importance of the Nile was reflected in the language of the ancient Egyptian. The word for travel whether on the desert or river was either "Khed," meaning "to go downstream," or "Khent" meaning "to go upstream." The river was the only easily accessible way to go from one part of Egypt to another part.

At least 4,000 years ago, the ancient Egyptians learned to move freely up and down the

Figure 20

Boats on the Nile, c. 2500 B.C.

Figure 21

Boats on the Nile, c. 2500 B.C.

Nile using the prevailing summer winds. They used what scientists now call the Etesian winds to move their sailboats.

Etesian winds blow across the Mediterranean Sea into Egypt during the summer. The winds develop because the air over the desert in the south is much warmer than air over the Nile delta. The cooler Etesian winds stay near the ground as they blow southward up the Nile. Meanwhile, the hot desert air rises from the south and above the cooler air. The Etesian winds blow from May until October and can reach speeds up to 40 miles an hour.

The ancient Egyptians used the Nile's natural current to carry their boats and ships northward down the river toward the sea. They used the Etesian winds to push their vessels south and upstream, towards Karnak or Aswan. These expert boatmen solved a problem that other river civilizations had much greater trouble comprehending — how to carry goods upstream, against the current.

The ease and swiftness of river travel increased the empire's prosperity. Merchants were active up and down the Nile. Tiny villages along the Nile's banks became active centers of commerce further establishing civilization in ancient Egypt.

Trade with other nations increased. Soon, larger ships were needed and ways to propel these ships were needed so that they would not be hostage to the winds or currents.

Cecil Torr, author of the book *Ancient Ships*, says that ''the art of rowing can first be discerned along the Nile'' (c. 2500 B.C.).

The museum at Palermo, Italy has in its possession a piece of hard, black, diorite tablet on which the following message is inscribed ''we brought 40 ships, laden with cedar trunks. We built ships of cedarwood — one 'Pride of Two Lands,' a ship of 150 feet — and of meru wood, two ships 150 feet long. We made the doors of the King's palace of cedarwood.'' That is the gist of the message from an Egyptian importer's records written during the reign of Pharaoh Snefru about 2700 B.C. He sent a fleet of ships to what is now Lebanon, to obtain wood to build ships for his navy. In war as well as peace Egyptian prowess upon the sea was demonstrated in several instances.

Ahmose, an officer in the Royal Egyptian Navy left posterity a record of a decisive naval battle on the walls of his tomb at El Kab. During the battles to drive the hated Hyksos from Egypt, groups of royal military galleys were sent north down the Nile. From the walls of his tomb, Ahmose says ''Avaris (the enemy commander) was taken: I captured one man and three women, four people in all.'' ... ''Sharuhen (a city) was besieged for three years before his majesty captured it... I was given gold for my bravery as well as prisoners for my slaves.'' All this took place in 1580 B.C.

In the eighth year of the reign of Rameses III (1188 B.C.) Egypt mobilized its Navy as the threat of invasion by the Philistines and other ''Peoples of the Sea'' grew imminent. West of Thebes (Waset) in Medinet Habu the ruins of the temple of Amon carry on its walls a record of the preparations for war.

Rameses III according to the inscriptions ''turned the river mouths into a strong defensive wall, with warships, galleys and coastal vessels... fully manned from stem to stern with brave warriors armed to the teeth.'' After slaughtering the Philistines on land the Pharaoh rushed his forces to the banks of the Nile to view what they hoped would be still another victory.

The opposing fleets slowly approached each other; suddenly their sails went slack. The ships had been beset by a calm. This circumstance was to the advantage of the Egyptians. The Philistine ships were fully dependent on wind and sail. The North Africans had oarsmen. An order was passed and the oarsmen rowed to a safe distance. Then the Egyptian archers were ordered to open fire. A hail of arrows struck the packed enemy ships and a frightful slaughter took place.

The Philistine soldiers and sailors who cheated death by jumping overboard were killed or captured by Egyptian forces once they reached the shore. It was the greatest naval victory that had ever occurred on the Nile. A post battle body count was made of the dead by slicing off the hands of the Philistines and piling them in heaps. The remaining prisoners were placed in P.O.W. camps after the Pharaoh's name had been branded on their skins.

A growing body of data is steadily being accumulated to prove that ancient Egyptians were also competent shipwrights. Approximately 2700 years before the Christian era, the people of the Nile discovered how to construct sleek wooden ships with hollow hulls and cabins and decks of closely fitted timbers. Temple reliefs, paintings, and surviving documents attest to the kingdom's shipbuilding skill.

In *Life in Ancient Egypt*, Adolph Erman remarked that given the Egyptian's reliance on the Nile ''it was natural that the building of river boats should be early developed as a national art.'' He described the preparations of boats as ''excellent.''

In 1954 a spectacular discovery of two undisturbed boat graves was made close to the Great Pyramid of Khufu. Inside one of the graves, hermetically sealed with hugh stone slabs was a disassembled ship made of 1,224 parts of cedar wood 4,600 years ago. When the vessel was completely assembled the result was a ship over 140 feet long. The Norwegian anthropologist Thor Heyerdahl described the vessel as ''perfectly streamlined and elegant.''

In the April 1988 edition of *National Geographic* magazine, Farouk El-Baz recounted how a team of scientists with high-tech equipment investigated the second boat grave over three decades later. Using a special drill, a remote controlled video camera, and environmental sensing equipment, scientists bored a small hole through a 15-ton, six foot thick covering slab. They viewed the disabled parts of a graceful wooden papyriform boat similar to the first one.

The condition of its second boat was worse because of water damage. Efforts to obtain samples of ancient air from the pit failed. The construction of a museum to house the first boat above ground had unintentionally broken the air tight seal of the second pit.

Both boat graves were discovered on the south side of the Great Pyramid. Remains of three other boat graves were found about a century ago on the east side of the Great Pyramid. Khufu's son, Djedefre, has boat graves surrounding his pyramid at Abu Ruwash. Khafre, builder of the second largest pyramid at Giza, and several royal wives buried there are among the ancient rulers with boat graves around their final resting places.

Long after the Pyramid Age, boats continued to figure in the funerary rites of the pharaohs. Oars were found in the corridor leading to Pharaoh Tutankhamen's burial chamber. Also among his tomb goods were several models of boats, including a copy of one he probably used during his lifetime. There is also a beautifully sculptured alabaster scent container in the shape of a boat. The exact purpose of these buried boats and nautical artifacts is not agreed upon by experts. Most believe that at least symbolically, the boats played a role in funerary rituals.

Egyptian boatbuilders carefully cut, trimmed, bored and framed the wood for each sailing vessel. They slowly and arduously bent each boat into a curve to give it a shallow draft. Boats for nobles were painted in various colors and often decorated with carved prows or inlaid woods. Royal boats had carried names like "Star of the Two Countries" or "Fame of 'Esse'." War boats were sometimes named "Glorious in Memphis," "Beloved of Amon," or "Battle Animal." There were only minor changes in boat building techniques and styles from the Old Kingdom to the New Kingdom. Although deck space would be cramped according to modern standards, the Egyptians shipped an impressive array of goods on the decks of a large variety of water craft.

In the tomb of Huy, the viceroy of Nubia during the reign of Pharaoh Tutankhamen, there is a drawing of the boat in which he sailed to his headquarters. The boat has a large cabin in the center of the deck, and there are cabins fore and aft bearing figures representing the four Horuses of Nubia. Also on the main deck are box stalls with horses in them. The hull is decorated with the picture of the Pharaoh in the form of a sphinx subduing a Nubian.

There were also sailing boats, freight boats, war boats and tow boats. The oldest and most numerous type of boat, however, was made of papyrus. These small, light boats or skiffs, made of bundles of plants roped together, were the vessels of the common people. Most papyrus boats only held one or two people. Larger papyrus boats would safely transport an ox. By the end of the Old Kingdom, a papyrus boat large enough to hold over 30 oarsmen sailed the Nile.

Even the flimsy papyrus boats were proven capable of making long voyages in such diverse locations as the Atlantic and Indian Oceans. Thor Heyerdahl demonstrated such a possibility with his Ra Expeditions. He used papyrus boats constructed in Africa to sail to the Americas. The papyrus boats of the Ra Expeditions, carried to the Americas as would most African ships by the swift Canary and North Equatorial currents made their respective voyages in fairly good time.

RaI traveled from Safi in Morocco to Barbados in the Caribbean, about three thousand miles in eight weeks. RaII made the same voyage in fifty-seven days. Compare this with Columbus' time of 69 days for his first voyage or the trip of the Black captain and businessman Paul Cuffe in 1815 as he took thirty-eight Blacks (in a personally financed colonization attempt) from Massachusetts to Sierra Leone in fifty-seven days.

In addition to sailing the Nile, ancient Egyptians sailed their papyrus boats on the "Great Green" (Mediterranean Sea) and elsewhere. Pliny, in *Historica Naturalis*, quoted the third chief librarian of Alexandria, Erastosthenes, in a geographical description of Ceylon. Erastosthenes also reported that papyrus ships with the same sails and rigging as on the Nile sailed as far as Ceylon and the mouth of the Ganges River in India.

Over the centuries, a bustling trade developed between Egypt and eastern Africa. During the reign of Pharaoh Sahure around 2600 B.C., his scribes recorded the dispatch of his fleet to the land of Punt. Scholars differ over Punt's exact location in East Africa. Sahure's ships brought back 80,000 measures of myrrh, 6,000 measures of electrum (a

Figure 22

Egyptian ships during the time of Pharoah Hatshepsut, c. 1500 B.C.

combination of gold and silver often used to cap pyramids and obelisks), 2,600 measures of wood, and 23,020 measures of oil.

A thousand years later, Pharaoh Hatshepsut ordered that the routes to Punt be re-explored and trade relations be reopened with African ports on the Red Sea. One of a handful of females to rule Egypt, she sent out a flotilla of ships in the ninth year of her reign. A canal had been constructed from the eastern part of the Nile delta and into the Red Sea. It was this route that she ordered her admiral Nehesi and his sailors to take to reach Punt. According to Theodore Davis and his book, *Tomb of Hatshopsitu*, Nehesi means Negro or Nubian.

Once there, the Egyptians exchanged their native products for a priceless cargo of ebony, myrrh trees, aromatic woods, spices, herbs, gold, and apes. A complete record of the excursion was painted on Hatshepsut's magnificent tomb at Dier-el-Bahri.

East Africans were also engaged in trade with the peoples of southwest Asia at this time. Clay tablets found in the ancient city of "Ur of the Chaldees" birthplace of the Hebrew patriarch Abraham, list the receipt of red gold, lapis lazuli, and ivory. None of these products was native to that part of Asia. Archeologists and historians thought the evidence hinted at the existence of a long distance sailing and trading network involving the Horn of Africa, Asia and India. In 1977, Thor Heyerdahl helped confirm their suspicions by building a reed boat in Iraq and sailing it from there to East Africa. On the way he stopped in Bahrain on the Persian Gulf, and Mohenjo-Daro on the Indus River.

The *Bible* tells us that Israel during the reign of Solomon also carried on a thriving trade with East Africa. In the first book of Kings (9:28 & 10:11&22) trade with Ophir (East Africa) is mentioned. African sailors are mentioned in Isaiah (18:1&2).

African sailors and merchants continued their mercantilist practices well into the centuries after Christ. This is supported by the fact that Adulis, the Red Sea port of Ethiopia is mentioned in a Greek sailing guide called the *Periplus of the Erythrean Sea*, written in the second century A.D. Greeks and Romans of that period called the East African coast "Azania." The author of the Periplus describes an active trade with the Africans exchanging their raw materials for manufactured goods. The southernmost port of "Rhapta" is mentioned and is now believed to have been in Tanzania.

In the tenth century A.D. an Arab, al-Masudi further chronicled the affairs of seagoing East Africans. This was followed in the fourteenth century by the works of Ibn Battuta. The Arabs called this area the "Land of the Zanj."

These writers and others commented on the increasing scope and vitality of the East African maritime trade. By the fourteenth century, there was a strip of at least forty trading settlements extending down 2,000 miles of coastline. Some historians call this area the Swahili Corridor.

Swahili, the great trading language that grew out of the blending of Bantu and Arabic languages, was spoken all along the corridor at this time.

East African merchants traded with groups living in the interior for such things as ambergris, slaves, gold, rock crystal, copper and most importantly, ivory. Arab and African sailors took these goods to India, Persia, China, Basra in Iraq, or to Alexandria in Egypt. From there these cargoes found their way to Europe. In this way, these African materials

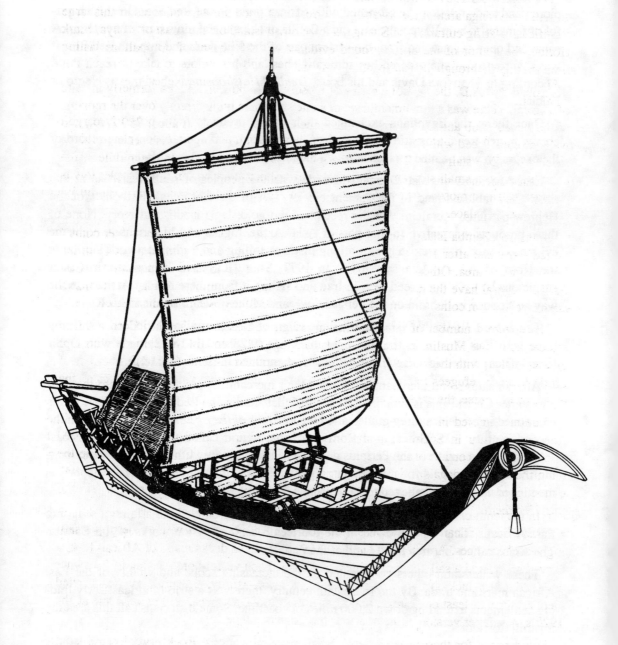

Figure 23

Mtepe

became mediums of expression for European artists during the Renaissance. Half a continent away, Chinese pottery was carried back to East Africa. This was trade on an international scale with diverse cultures mingling with and enriching each other.

The September 1987 edition of *Scientific American* reported that a series of excavations around the Shanga area of the Swahili Corridor, confirmed the African roots of this large "unified seafaring culture." At Shanga, a town on an island off the coast of Kenya, Mark Horton, the author of the article, found evidence of "25 phases of occupations lasting from the eighth through the fourteenth centuries."

Around 800 A.D. the first of a series of mosques was built in an area formerly the site of a corral. There was a monumental set of stone structures lying directly over the remains of the ruined daub and mud corral. "The stone complex, erected in about 950 A.D., had walls of coral faced with fine lime plaster. The buildings were on a lavish scale and were entered by stone stairways. They were surrounded by a stone wall... In the middle of the complex stood a small stone mosque capable of holding no more than 40 people; this is the earliest stone mosque known in sub-Saharan Africa." Horton compares these buildings to a royal palace.

On nearby Pemba Island, Horton discovered a cache of 2,000 "gold and silver coins" buried sometime after 1066 A.D. Some are Muslim designed and minted coins from the Mediterranean area. Others in the group are copies believed to have been minted in East Africa. Several have the names of local African rulers on them. At Manda, on the mainland, five Muslim coins, known to have been minted in Sicily, were also discovered.

There were a number of reasons Muslim traders settled in the Swahili Corridor. The relocation of the Muslim capital to Bagdad in 750 A.D. brought the entire region into greater contact with the Indian Ocean trading system, the resettlement of large numbers of Shiite Muslim refugees fleeing southern Arabia, the impressive natural resources of the area, and of course, the existing lucrative trade network.

As Horton noted in his article, "By the eighth century rapid sea travel was possible from Mogadishu in Somalia all the way to Mozambique, a distance of some 3,000 kilometers. The corridor was not easy to sail. The Mozambique Channel, separating the mainland from Madagascar, is dangerous, and the seasonal monsoons are unreliable south of the Equator. Along this route specialized navigators were needed and the Swahili provided them."

These East African traders moved their goods in Arab dhows as well as their own sailing vessels, mtepes. An mtepe might be 40 feet long, have decks made of African teak, a curved prow, and a sail made of matted palm leaf. Each vessel bore the flag of its owner and had good luck symbols painted on it. Simple, sturdy, graceful, mtepes carried elephants and at least one giraffe to China, iron to India, and were still used as late as the 1920's. A smaller version of the boat was the "dau la mtepe."

The cargoes for these vessels came from various locations. Rock crystal came from Ethiopia. Gold came from southern Africa. Ivory from San nomads, six hundred miles away on the fringes of the Kalihari Desert, ended up on the coast after being turned over in the trade chain several times; from hunter to herder to merchant to mariner each deriving an equitable benefit from the exchange. Key links in this rich trade were coastal towns that sprung up to serve as depots and markets.

Mogadishu, Malindi, Shanga, Manda, Pemba Island, Zanzibar, Mombasa, Sofala and Lamu are among the more famous towns. The residents of Lamu say it was the home port for one of the most famous adventurers in world literature, Sinbad the Sailor.

Kilwa was the greatest of these towns eclipsing Mogadishu, the older and northernmost site. Ibn Battuta called Kilwa, "the principal town on the coast, the greater part of whose inhabitants are Zanj of very Black complexion." And while he had also visited Mogadishu and Mombasa, Battuta described Kilwa as "one of the most beautiful and well-constructed towns in the world. The whole of it is elegantly built. The roofs are built with mangrove poles. There is very much rain. The people are engaged in a holy war; for their country lies beside that of pagan Zanj. The chief qualities are devotion and piety; they follow the Shafi'i rite."

During Battuta's visit in 1331, he recorded that the leader of Kilwa was Sultan Abu al-Mawahib ('the Father of Gifts'). "He was called this on account of his numerous charitable gifts." Battuta was pleased to report this. The sultan had been quite generous with him as well. Battuta had once criticized Mansa Sulayman, the emperor of Mali for being too stingy toward him. Battuta was used to being received in style and luxury when he visited the courts of the wealthy and famous. The wealth and largess of the leaders in the Swahili Corridor did not have much longer to flourish. This "gilded age" of splendor and adventure was in its twilight. During the late 1490s, the Swahili Corridor was on the eve of its destruction.

In 1498, the Portuguese mariner Vasco da Gama, sailed around the southern tip of Africa into the Swahili Corridor. These foreigners were amazed at its vitality, extent and riches. The Portuguese had come this way hoping to outflank their Muslim competitors in North Africa and the Levant. They sought a safe route to the spices and jewels of the Indies. But first they had to negotiate the difficult currents of the Mozambique Channel and the coral reefs protecting the towns.

In an essay entitled *Negro Contributions to the Explorations of the Globe*, historian Ronald W. Davis writes "Only through the aid of an east African pilot, Ibn Madjid, did the tiny fleet realize its goal, he was a long-term resident of East Africa... the author of one of a collection of rahmani, or sets of nautical instructions for negotiating the capricious monsoon winds of the Indian Ocean, the key to successful communication between India and East Africa. Without the aid of such a person, da Gama's voyage almost certainly would not have been successful."

The Portuguese decided to take control of the Swahili Corridor by intimidation or force. They dropped anchor in the harbors of the largest towns and offered a simple proposition: surrender and pay tribute to the King of Portugal or die. These peacetime competitors proved unable to mount a coordinated defense.

Malindi surrendered first. Outraged, the sultan of Mombasa declared war on the town. By 1505 Portuguese ships were raiding the trading towns and capturing ships. Francisco d'Almeida led a squadron of eleven Portuguese war ships with orders to subdue Barawa, Kilwa, and Mombasa.

What follows are actual Portuguese descriptions of the taking of Mombasa and Kilwa:

> From our ships the fine houses, terraces, and minarets, with the palms
> and trees in the orchards, made the city (Kilwa) look so beautiful that our

men were eager to land and overcome the pride of this barbarian, who spent all night bringing into the island archers from the mainlands [a local mainland ruler and trading partner sent his men to help protect the city. After a brutal street by street battle, the Portuguese seized Kilwa]... Then the Vicar-General and some of the Franciscan fathers came ashore carrying two crosses in procession and singing the Te Deum. They went to the palace; and there the cross was put down and [Captain Almeida] prayed. Then everyone started to plunder the town of its merchandise and provisions... [In less than three weeks, the Portuguese installed a new and more compliant ruler, refitted their ships, and attacked Mombasa.]

When we entered [the harbor] the first ship was fired on by the Moors [The Portuguese here used the name interchangeably with Muslim] from both sides. We promptly replied to the fire, and with such intensity that the gunpowder in their strong point caught fire. It started burning and the Moors fled, thus allowing the whole fleet to enter and lie at anchor in front of the town... when they went to burn the town they were received by the Moors with a shower of arrows and stones. The town has more than 600 houses which are thatched with palm leaves... In between the stone dwelling houses there are wooden houses with porches and stables for cattle. There are very few dwelling houses which have not these wooden houses attached. Once the fire started it raged all night long... It was a moonless night. [Early the next day, covered by groups of archers and musketeers, the Portuguese entered Mombasa, encountering brief, ineffective resistance. Four Portuguese soldiers died. The visitors estimated they had killed over 1500 Africans.]

The Grand Captain ordered that the town should be sacked and that each man should carry off to his ship whatever he found so that at the end there would be a division of the spoil, each man to receive a twentieth of what he found. The same rule was made for gold, silver, and pearls. Then everyone started to plunder the town and to search the houses, forcing open the doors with axes and iron bars... A large quantity of rich silk and gold embroidered clothes was seized and carpets also; one of these, which was without equal for beauty, was sent to the King of Portugal together with many other valuables.

Due to continuing opposition, Mombasa was sacked again in 1528 and 1589. In order to finally put down resistance along the corridor, the Portuguese erected in 1593 a massive stronghold ironically named Fort Jesus. On Mozambique, they built Fort St. Sebastian. Forts were also built on Kilwa and at Sofala.

The Swahili Corridor was closed.

Over two thousand years earlier, on the rim of the continent, North African sailors established what many historians consider the first great sea power in the Mediterranean — Khart Hadasht or Carthago as the Romans called it. Today we know it as Carthage. Its original name means "new town." It stood near the modern city of Tunis.

Carthage was originally a small colony founded by Phoenicians around 800 B.C. The

Figure 24
Phoenician/Carthaginian vessels, c. 600 B.C.

Phoenicians were seagoing Semitic speaking people, searching for precious metals and trading opportunities. British military historian Terrence Wise describes them as Canaanites from the city of Tyre in ancient Palestine. The Greeks, he says, called them Phoenicians which means "dark skinned."

The settlers freely intermingled with the local African population of herders and farmers. An impressive and expansive mercantile city-state developed in which an aristocratic upper house or senate jointly ruled with a citizens assembly elected by property owners. Two kings were elected annually.

It is possible to gain some general idea of the physical appearance of the Carthaginians. An African born in Leptis Magna, originally a Carthaginian colony, became a Roman emperor. His name was Lucius Septimius Severus (146 A.D.-211 A.D.).

By 500 B.C. Carthage had risen to become the unchallenged power in the Mediterranean Sea. Carthage established settlements in Spain and Gaul. She seized ships of every potential competitor that she could catch west of Sardinia, fought the Greeks for possession of Sicily, suppressed piracy, and had a considerable land trade across the Sahara with West Africa. The principal commodities were salt, gold, copper, cloth, various stones, ivory and slaves. Today, in the Tassili Mountains of the Central Sahara there are rock paintings dating from this time and showing two-wheeled horse drawn chariots dashing across the desert. Carthaginians traded and worked Spanish copper and sailed to England to obtain tin. Carthaginian coins and tools have been found on the Scilly Isles off the English coast.

The symbol of the Carthaginian monopoly on trade in the western Mediterranean was the Pillars of Melkart later called by the Greeks the Pillars of Hercules. Also called Calpe and Abyla, these two huge rocky headlands were supposedly bound together until Melkart (Hercules) pulled them apart. According to the legend, the Phoenicians were said to have built on each headland two large pyramidal columns that functioned as seamarks. One was dedicated to Ashtoreth, the goddess of fertility. The other dedicated to Melkart.

The rocks on which the pillars stood represented the utmost limits of the known world. The Carthaginians never let anyone sail beyond, that is except themselves. They are believed to have visited Madeira, the Canary Islands and possibly the Azores.

About 520 B.C. a Carthaginian sailor named Hanno sailed past the pillars and according to his journal, the *Periplus of Hanno*, sailed along the coast of West Africa (see Chapter 1). Twenty years later Himilco, a Carthaginian sea captain, sailed to Europe, possibly reaching Ireland. According to the Roman poet Rufus Festus Avenius in *Ora Maritima*, Himilco may then have sailed into the Atlantic as far west as the Sargasso Sea.

In 265 B.C. the first Punic War began as Rome sought to topple Carthage from the pinnacle of power she had so long enjoyed. A series of bloody struggles of attrition on land and sea followed lasting well over a century. In 219 B.C. Carthage had an estimated population of one million. Eighteen miles of walls circled its courtyards, markets, palaces, and gardens. At the end of the third Punic War (146 B.C.), Rome was the dominant sea power in the Mediterranean and as revenge the city of Carthage was burnt, its remaining inhabitants sold into slavery. The ruins of the city were plowed under and a curse was invoked upon anyone attempting to rebuild it.

In 29 B.C. the Roman Emperor Augustus restored it to a semblance of its earlier glory. After surviving the Vandals and Byzantines, Carthage was destroyed again by the Arabs in 697 A.D.

Centuries later Africa raised yet another crop of fearless sailors. They were Moorish and Turkish sea rovers known as the Barbary Coast Pirates. The Barbary Coast is a region in Northern Africa extending from the western border of Egypt to the Atlantic Ocean. It included the states of Morocco, Algeria, Tunisia and Libya (Tripolitania). Arabs called the region, the "Maghreb," the West. For three hundred years these Moorish pirates brazenly sailed the Mediterranean at will. They even sailed out into the Atlantic and as far north as Scandinavia.

Their reign of terror peaked during the 17th century but their origins went back much further in time. Under the command of men like the coal black sultan Mulai Ismael (1672-1723), Empsael from the Sudan, and the Barbarossas, renegade Europeans; the pirates exacted tribute from all the Christian nations of Europe and the United States.

During the 17th century the Algerian and Tunisian corsairs (raiding ships) joined forces and in the first half of the century more than 20,000 white Christian captives were said to be imprisoned in Algiers alone. Thousands of English, Scotch, French, and Portuguese were sold into slavery in Africa or western Asia. One of Mulai Ismael's slaves was Alexander Selkirk, the hero of Robinson Crusoe.

In 1631, an expedition manned by the African pirates sacked Baltimore, Ireland and returned with white slaves and booty. The leader of the raid was a black man named Ali Krussa. Generations of Scottish children who misbehaved were threatened with the Mahound, a black devil who would take them away. This character was based on the depredations of the Barbary Coast pirates. There were several attempts to dislodge the pirates from their bases to Africa, among the best known were the assault of Charles V in 1541, the series of attacks by the French fleet under Admiral Duquesne (1682-1683), the Anglo-Dutch Punitive expedition in 1816 and the Tripolitanian War (1801-1805) and the war with Algiers (1815) between the United States and the Barbary Coast.

The region was called the Barbary Coast because the area had been originally occupied by a racially mixed group of Africans called Berbers. The tiny coastal states which encouraged and profited from the activities of these freebooters, were semi-independent vassals under the nominal authority of the Turkish Ottoman empire. Crews were often mixed. Africans, Arabs, Turks, and Greeks served together aboard these ships.

The conflict between the United States and the pirates began in 1801, when the United States refused the demand of Tripoli for a payment of $225,000 plus $23,000 annually. In 1795, the United States had bought peace from Algiers and Tunis by paying $800,000, supplying a frigate, and an annual tribute of $25,000. In effect, the United States paid protection money to Africans. An American punitive expedition was dispatched under Commodores Dale and Morris to Tripoli but they failed to decisively accomplish their mission. Another American officer, Commodore Preble did initiate a successful blockade against Tripoli. The pasha of Tripoli, further threatened with an attack by land as well as sea signed a treaty early in June 1805, by which the United States agreed to pay $60,000 for prisoners taken by the Tripolitanians in return for which the pasha agreed to forego any subsequent regular tribute.

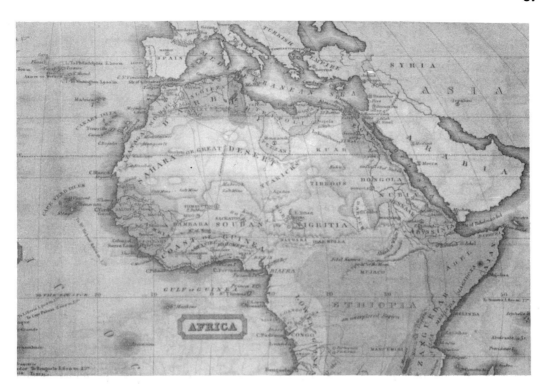

Figure 25

The Barbary Coast states

Figure 26

Christian slavery in Barbary

In the following years the United States, however, continued to pay tribute to the other Barbary States. President Jefferson's embargo of 1807 all but destroyed American commerce in the Mediterranean, but with the resumption of trade in 1810, the pirates continued their attacks.

In 1812, the dey of Algiers demanded more tribute and then issued a declaration of war but because of the War of 1812 there was virtually no American shipping to seize and ransom. Once the war was over the government dispatched a fleet under the command of Stephen Decatur who succeeded in forcibly making all the Barbary pirates adhere to a treaty relinquishing tributes, property, and Christian slaves. An American peace keeping force remained in the Mediterranean area to see that the terms of the treaty were carried out and to protect U.S. shipping. This signaled the end of major American difficulties with the pirates of the Barbary Coast. In the *Naval Battles of The United States*, printed in Boston in 1859, the importance of the Barbary Coast wars to the development of the United States Navy was explained:

> The depredations committed on our commerce in the Mediterranean, by the piratical corsairs of the Barbary powers, induced Congress in 1794, to undertake the formation of a naval force for its protection. Four ships, of forty-four guns each, and two of thirty-six were ordered to be built. The act authorizing the construction of these ships, passed the twenty-seventh day of March, which may be considered as the day that gave existence to the navy of the United States.

The pirates, however, continued to raid the European coastline with a fair amount of impunity until 1830. In that year French forces occupied Algiers and effectively subdued the pirates of North Africa. The activities of the Barbary Coast pirates influenced the history of the western world. Europe embarked on its age of exploration particularly to find another water route to India because, in part, the pirates had bottled up the shipping lanes of the Mediterranean.

The peoples of Central and West Africa primarily displayed their major sailing skills along the rivers framing the Zaire River (Congo) basin, in the Niger River system, and in the waters of smaller rivers such as the Gambia or the Senegal. Their larger vessels were usually immense dugout canoes made of hollowed out tree trunks which were nevertheless roomy, watertight, durable, and even sleek. They were finely suited for trade and travel.

The white explorer Henry Morton Stanley described the navy of the Kabaka Mutesa I of Buganda as consisting of over 300 carved and beautifully ornamented canoes, some over 70 feet long. Stanley became a keen judge of central African watercraft beginning in 1876 when he began his infamous descent of the Lualaba River in Zaire. Using the latest repeating rifles, he fought more than two dozen battles against poorly armed warriors that left his wake full of floating corpses.

In February 1877, Stanley fought a pitched battle with the fleet of the Mangbetu people near the junction of the Zaire (Congo) and Aruwimi Rivers. He noted that he was attacked by 54 huge canoes each with a crew of oarsmen handling ten-foot long brass bottomed paddles capped with ivory balls. The Mangbetu flagship carried ten officers and 40 oarsmen. The canoes carried a total of two thousand men. Master metal workers, each

Mangbetu warrior carried an assortment of lethal copper and brass spears, poniards, throwing knives, or axes.

During each assault the Mangbetu beat their huge drums, sounded their horns, and made their battle chants. They nearly cut Stanley's improvised fleet in half. Of their formidable courage, awesome weapons, and impressive tactics, he grudgingly wrote "the people on the banks of this river are clever, intelligent, and more advanced in the arts than any hitherto observed since we commenced our descent of the Livingstone." Stanley had singlehandedly renamed the Zaire (Congo) river in honor of the missionary he came to Africa to find in 1871.

Several early European explorers of West Africa recorded the existence of large dugout canoes in addition to smaller watercraft normally associated with so called premature cultures. About 1445 Dinis Dias and in 1455 Alvise da Cadamosto saw huge dugout canoes capable of carrying large numbers of men.

Cadamosto encountered dugout canoes propelled by oars and carrying "twenty-five to thirty negroes in each." He also later saw "two canoes which were similar to the ones already described and in truth were of a great size. One was almost as large as one of our vessels, but not so high and in it were more than 30 Negroes; the other was smaller, having about 16 men."

Further inland on the Niger River in 1796 the Scottish adventurer Mungo Park, observed in one large canoe "four horses and several people crossing over the river." In 1827, Rene Caillie, the first European to actually see and describe Timbuktu, recorded crossing a river "with our luggage and a canoe about fifty feet long and exceedingly narrow; it was formed of two trunks of trees united lengthwise and fashioned with cords..."

Near Timbuktu, Caillie saw an 80-boat flotilla with African boats 90 or 100 feet long, 12 or 14 feet across with shallow drafts. The vessels carried a variety of grains, cotton, honey and vegetable butter. He estimated one vessel was..." of sixty or eighty tons burden."

In 1836, Captain James Riley, the survivor of an 1815 shipwreck off the West African coast and a year's slavery in Africa, published his autobiography. In it he included an account of his former master-turned-friend Sidi Hamets' journeys to Timbuktu from Morocco in enormous camel caravans across the Sahara. Although Caillie some eleven or more years later found Timbuktu dusty and disappointing, Sidi Hamet was truly impressed with the city each time he saw it.

Calling Timbuktu "very rich, very large," Hamet remembered that the city:

> carries on a great trade with all the caravans that come from Morocco
> and the shores of the Mediterranean Sea. From Algiers, Tunis, Tripoli, &
> c. are brought all kinds of clothes, iron, salt, muskets, powder and lead,
> swords or scimitars, tobacco, opium, spices, and perfumes, amber beads,
> and other trinkets ... they carry back in return elephant's teeth, gold dust,
> and wrought gold, gum senegal, ostrich feathers, very curiously worked
> turbans, and slaves; a great many of the latter ...

Camped near the Niger River, Hamet saw large dugout canoes land near Timbuktu.

"Here," he told Riley, "we saw many boats made of great trees, some with Negroes in them paddling across the river."

Three weeks of camel back travel south of Timbuktu, Hamet entered another great trading city near the Niger. He called it Wassanah. He believed it was even larger than Timbuktu. Here as well, he noted the prosperity of the inhabitants. "They have boats made of great trees, cut off hollowed out, that will hold ten, fifteen, or twenty Negroes." The brothers of the King of Wassanah told one of Hamet's companions" ... that he was going to set out in a few days with sixty boats and to carry five hundred slaves down river... he said it was a long way and would take him three moons to get there." Hamet was also told there were between 300 and 400 boats in the river.

During the early years of slavery in the New World, west Africans brought their technology of single and multiple log dugout canoes to the Americas. Blending their skills with those of native American boat builders they created vessels called pirogues or periaguas. By themselves, Africans made dugouts called "poquoson," in the tidewater area of Virginia. They carried casks of tobacco in the Chesapeake Bay area, fish, or even pirates in the Caribbean.

In *Black Odyssey: The Seafaring Tradition of Afro-Americans*, James B. Farr describes how one black Caribbean pirate traded up a multiple log dugout he had fitted with a sail in order to get a larger ship. "A bold young Jamaican named Lewis," escaped imprisonment in Cuba with six other men. "Determined to join the ranks of buccaneers, the band first stole a small canoe and set out to find a more suitable vessel. They first seized a Spanish periagua, out of which several crewmen joined their captors." Lewis finally sailed under the skull and bones after taking a large French ship with two dozen guns and assembling a crew of 80, half of whom were black.

About 400 miles west of Dakar, Senegal is a cluster of islands that are home to another group of seafaring Africans. When the Portuguese first discovered these uninhabited islands in 1460, they called them Cabo Verde, the "Green Cape" after the western cape of Africa. Soon immigrants from Portugal, Spain, and Italy arrived. A short time later many African slaves arrived. Today's inhabitants derive from a blending of those groups. About 71 percent of the islanders are Creole (Mulatto). Unmixed Africans make up 28 percent of the population; approximately one percent is European.

Throughout the 1400s, the Cape Verde Islands served as the final friendly landfall or map reference point before the long voyage across the Atlantic Ocean. Columbus, Cabral, Magellan, and da Gama put into the Cape Verde islands for supplies or refitting before beginning the major parts of their journeys. Charles Darwin and his ship stopped there in 1832. Many Cape Verdeans were naturally drawn to the sea. They served as cooks, stewards, and able bodied seamen aboard the vessels of many nations. A number of Cape Verdeans, sometimes called "Bravas" or "black Portuguese" came to the United States on whaling ships in the late 1700s and early 1800s settling in and around New Bedford, Massachusetts, then the nation's whaling center. Today, the New Bedford community is still home to the largest concentration of Cape Verdeans in the United States.

Several Cape Verdeans sailed their own ships to America. Captain Henry Mendes crossed the Atlantic over fifty times in his ship "Ernestina." He brought thousands of his countrymen to the United States. Today, the Ernestina rests at anchor in New Bedford harbor serving as a visible symbol of the Cape Verdean link to the sea.

Africans were among the world's great sailors. Their skill, daring and enterprise took them far and wide across the seas and oceans. African sailors, using a variety of watercraft, touched far off shores and carried their culture and boldness to every part of both the old world and the new world.

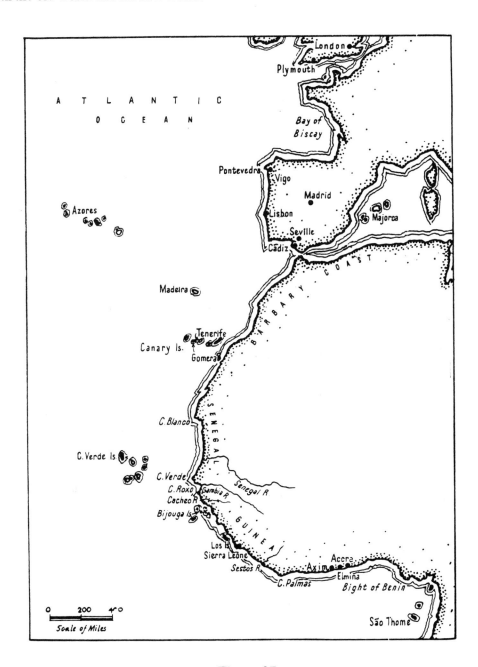

Figure 27

Map of the West African coast

CHAPTER 3

AFRICAN EXPLORATION OF THE AMERICAS

THE TIME BEFORE COLUMBUS

The voyages of Columbus more than others have been used as a yardstick by many historians to measure the successes and failures of other explorers. The magic of the Columbus myth — his being the "first to discover America" — still lives in the textbooks and hearts of many American children.

Today, of course, we know there are other claimants to the title, which has changed from discoverer of America — for the Native American is unchallenged there — to the first non-Native American or even first European. The Viking Lief Erikson is believed to have sailed from Greenland to Newfoundland around 1001 A.D.

Others believe that the Irish monk, St. Brendan, reached North America sometime during the sixth century A.D. And there is the 40-year voyage the Chinese Buddhist monk Huishen made along the California Coast around 498 A.D. He lived with the Indians in what he called "the wonderful land of Fusang." He reported his voyage in the year of Yung Yuan during the Ch'i dynasty.

Nowhere among these traditional and competing clarions of voyages of discovery is the African considered. Even today it seems that many people hold the view of individuals like Dr. William Draper. In the first edition of his book, *History of the Intellectual Development of Europe* published in 1861 in New York, he classed West African blacks as impotent, land-bound savages incapable of undertaking a transatlantic voyage. The 1976 Bicentennial edition of the *Encyclopedia of American History* flatly dismissed the idea of a pre-Columbian African presence in America.

Carter G. Woodson, the "father of Negro History," knew such an attitude was patently false. For years there had been unconnected bits of evidence and various hypotheses suggesting that Africans had arrived in the Americas before Columbus. In fact, from shortly after the publication of Draper's book through the turn of the century, there was a series of discoveries that would finally begin to erase any doubt of African presence in the New World before Columbus.

Many early 19th century white historians and writers including Leo Frobenius, Lewis Spence, Albert Churchward, Gerald Massey, Grafton Elliot Smith, and Flora Shaw Lugard provided information on ancient African influences in pre-Columbian America.

By the early years of this century, Woodson was moved to write in *The Negro In Our History*,

> Inasmuch as scientists now claim there once existed on the western coast of Africa a very advanced people who influenced even the civilization of the Mediterranean world, they have little doubt of their having extended their culture across the middle passage. Africa, it will be remembered, is nearer to America than Europe.

There is considerable evidence to place the African presence in the Americas especially Mexico to a period before Columbus and possibly back to the times of the pharaohs of Egypt. The similarities between the civilizations of the Mayas, Incas, Aztecs and Egyptians are truly remarkable. In the January 1966 issue of the magazine *American Antiquity*, John Howland Rowe, a University of California anthropologist, compiled a list of 60 special features of a uniquely distinctive nature and limited world distribution which were characteristic of both the ancient cultures of the Eastern Mediterranean and pre-Columbian Peru, Ecuador, and Colombia.

The pyramids are perhaps the most striking similarities. There are those who say the theory of early contact is not valid because American pyramids are stepped while the Egyptian pyramids are smooth-sided. These isolationists forget the simple historical fact that the earliest pyramids in Egypt, those of the third and early fourth dynasty, c.2600 B.C., are stepped.

Many isolationist historians claim that Egyptians lacked the necessary skill to negotiate a trans-Atlantic crossing. Chapter Two of this book provides ample evidence of African long distance sailing ability and accomplishments.

In 1976, two books were published that sounded the death knell for those who claimed that Africans could never have sailed across the Atlantic. In *They Came Before Columbus*, professor Ivan Van Sertima presented a catalog of documents, carvings, obscure scientific works, and botanical and other data to prove not only that pharaonic-period Africans sailed to the Americas but were a major influence on the Olmec civilization, the mother culture of all the native cultures of Meso-America. Van Sertima ended his book with ''...therefore it can only be concluded that Atlantic migration from the African continent is responsible for the black pre-Columbian presence in America from the Olmecs onward.''

Harvard professor Barry Fell in *America, B.C.* assembled a host of temple inscriptions, petroglyphs, gravestones, tablets, ancient rock shelters, little known writing systems, and various other artifacts and concluded that many ancient peoples including Africans visited the Americas. He also believes that Scandinavians and Sumerians may have visited America as early as 5,000 B.C. to 3,000 B.C. Some of these ancient visitors were also Greeks, Romans, Phoenicians, and Celts.

From 1500 B.C. onward, Fell's data indicate there were African contacts ''with Indian natives of the northeast.'' Much of the existing Algonquin Indian words used in legal matters, treatment of illness and sailing stems from these ancient encounters, according to Fell. He believes that the writing system of the Micmac, a Native American people of the Canadian maritime provinces and Newfoundland, is based on Egyptian hieroglyphics. His research suggests that between 500 B.C. and 179 B.C. there was regular trade between Africa and North America.

According to most scholars, however, the classic work on the African presence in America is *Africa in the Discovery of America*. It is a three-volume master work published between 1920 and 1922 by Professor Leo Wiener of Harvard University. Wiener wrote volume one in 1920. He subsequently finished two other volumes (Nos. 2 and 3) about two years later. Wiener, a philologist, was researching Native American linguistic origins and determined somewhat incredulously that there was a considerable African influence in many of the languages.

In Wiener's first volume he wrote that based upon his studies ''Negroes have had a far greater influence upon American civilization than has heretofore been suspected.'' He also forecast what material his second volume would cover at this same time. ''I shall show by documentary evidence to what extraordinary extent the Indian medicine-man owes his evolution to the African medicine-man.''

Wiener's third volume delved into the areas of social and religious contact between Africans and pre-Columbian Indian American societies. On page 365 Wiener stated: "the presence of Negroes with their trading masters in America before Columbus is proved by the representation of Negroes in American sculpture and design, by the occurrence of a black nation at Darien early in the XVI century, but more specifically by Columbus' emphatic reference to Negro traders from Guinea, who trafficked in a gold alloy, "guanin" of precisely the same composition having the same name as frequently referred to by early writers in Africa."

Wiener noted in the same volume that West Africans had landed in several locations in North and South America. He further wrote that "There were several foci from which the Negro traders spread into the two Americas. The eastern part of South America where the Caribs are mentioned seems to have been reached by them from the West Indies. Another stream, possibly from the same focus, radiated to the north along roads marked by the presence of mounds, and reached as far as Canada. The chief culture influence was exerted by a Negro colony in Mexico, most likely from Teotihuacan and Tuxtla, who may have been instrumental in establishing the city of Mexico. From here their influence pervaded the neighboring tribes and ultimately, directly or indirectly, reached Peru."

Also in this volume, Wiener shows how closely a Central American Indian astrological artifact, the "Plate of the Bacabs" resembles an Arabic astrological artifact called a "gadwal." The gadwal was in wide use throughout Western Africa. Wiener found a series of similarities between the artifacts and links them to similar representations in the Mound Builders Culture. He attributes an African influence to the Native American manifestations of complex, spiritual beliefs.

These revelations merely supported his philological studies done two years previously in Volume I, for at that time he explored the existence of West African crops and words in Native American languages. On page 262 of Volume I, Wiener argued that "Indeed when we turn to the appellations of the sweet potato and yam in America, we find nothing but African forms. Here as there, the two are confounded, and chiefly those names have survived which Dr. Chanca mentioned in 1494. He called the plant he described, apparently the sweet potato, both nabi and hage. We see that the first is a phonetic variation of Wolof Nyambi, etc., 'Yam.' " Wiener believed that Native American words such as canoe and tobacco were of African origin.

Professor Weiner was not the lone advocate of Africa's early presence in America. In 1900, Peter DeRoo wrote in *History of America Before Columbus*, "Yet a better proof of ancient Negro arrivals is the fact of Negro colonies found by Spanish and Portuguese discoverers on the eastern coast of South and Central America. Mendoza encountered a tribe of Negroes, and Balboa, went on his famous expeditions of the discovery of the Pacific Ocean, met in the old province of Quareca, and only two days travel from the Gulf of Darien, with a settlement of Negroes."

In *Africa's Gifts to America*, J.A. Rogers quoted several Hispanic scholars on the African presence in the Americas." C.C. Marquez says, "The type is seen in the most ancient Mexican sculpture...Negroes figure frequently in the most remote traditions. A colleague of Marquez, Rima Palacio stated "It is indisputable that in very ancient times the

Negro race occupied our territory (Mexico). The Mexicans recall a Negro god, Ixtilton, which means 'black face.' ''

Since the final decade of the last century, hard, indisputable archaeological evidence has cropped up to support the theories of those historians. The most thought provoking and mysterious material has been the artifacts left behind by the Olmec civilization (pre-Aztec) in Mexico.

The exact arrival of these people is in doubt. V.W. Von Hagen, author of *The Aztec: Man and Tribe*, thinks the Olmecs arrived around 1000 B.C. in the Vera Cruz-Tabasco area of Mexico:

> In Aztec mytho-history, Olmecs were known as the people who lived in the direction of the rising sun and a glyph history of them shows that their paradisiacal ''wealth'' consisted of rubber, pitch, jade, chocolate, and bird feathers. We do not know what they called themselves. Olmec derives from olli (rubber) ... They traded rubber and they presumably made the rubber balls used for the game called Tlachtli. A talented and mysterious people ... they were centered about the Coatzacoalocs River basin on the Gulf Coast ... Only in recent times have the great Olmec stone heads been unearthed by Dr. Matthew Stirling. At Tres Zapotes he found one colossal head seven feet high, flat nosed and sensually thick lipped.

The first of the huge heads many of them weighing several tons, was discovered near Vera Cruz by Jose M. Melgar y Serrano. Melgar published a monograph on his findings in 1869 (and 1871) in which he describes the massive sculpture as having ''Ethiopian features.'' Near the Gulf of Mexico, in 1902, an Olmec figurine was found that dated back as far as 98 B.C. A green jadette carving of an Indian priest, the figurine is believed to be the work of the Olmec even though it bears Mayan-like glyphs. A party of archeologists from Tulane University discovered an Olmec head in 1925 but did not unearth it.

Stirling led nine expeditions into the Mexico Gulf coastal region. The second expedition in 1939 discovered five heads in LaVenta in the state of Tabasco, five to nine feet high weighing 20 to 30 tons each. Stirling published his findings during World War II. After the war, he returned to Mexico to locate other huge stone heads.

One of the most famous heads was discovered on a small hill a few miles north of Tres Zapotes. In 1951 it was taken from there to the town of Santiago Tuxtla, Vera Cruz. This ''cabeza colosal,'' its Mexican nickname, was placed on one edge of the village plaza. Archeologists call it Tres Zapotes Colossal Head No. 2. The giant head is five feet high, four feet two inches wide, and eleven feet in circumference. And it weighs 8.5 short tons. It has the same military style headgear as most of the other heads. On the back of the head are representations of seven braids or cornrows, hanging vertically with each end adorned with a button or rosette. A description of the head in the July 1965 issue of *American Antiquity* called it ''unusual with respect to its marked prognathism'' (a jutting out of the lower jaw characteristic of some African facial types).

In 1967, a group from Yale University ventured into the Tres Zapotes area and excavated another huge head with unmistakably African features. This find made the cover of *Science Digest* for September of that year and inspired a companion article.

Figure 28

Tres Zapotes Colossal Head No. 2

Figure 29

Tres Zapotes Colossal Head No. 2

Terra Cotta sculptures with unmistakeably African physiognomies have also been unearthed in the Mexican provinces of Guerrero, Chiapas, Tabasco, and the Central Plateau of Mexico.

It is imperative that we also examine what impelled the West African to conquer the Atlantic and what further proof is offered by historians. The West African kingdoms of Ghana, Mali and Songhay flourished before, during and after Europe's "Dark Ages." Their levels of culture, socio-economic stability and prosperity were admired by many travelers and writers including Leo Africanus, William Bosman and Ibn Battuta. (This was before the rationalization of the slave trade made it soothing to the conscience to portray Africans as savages.)

Harold G. Lawrence in a 1962 edition of *Crisis* Magazine unequivocally indicates that "we can now positively state that the Mandingoes of the Mali and Songhay Empires, and possibly other Africans, crossed the Atlantic to carry on trade with the Western Hemisphere Indians and further succeeded in establishing colonies throughout the Americas." Lawrence goes on to say that due to diplomatic relations with Morocco the Malian Emperor Sakura (1285 — 1300 A.D.) learned advanced nautical technology and the spherical nature of the earth. Various Arab scholars, some of whom were Abulfeda, Idrisi, Abu Zaid and Abul Wafa developed geographics and astronomical theories. Some historians believe the West African rulers wanted to test these theories first hand.

In his book, *Africans and Their History*, J.E. Harris writes that Abubakari II (1305-1311) sent a fleet of two hundred ships into the Atlantic informing the captains not to return until they had found land or run out of supplies. One vessel returned after a considerable passage of time and reported the others lost at sea. Abubakari himself led a second expedition of two hundred ships leaving his brother Mansa Musa in power. Abubakari never returned to claim his throne and that is all we know of those voyages.

In *The Lost Cities of Africa*, Basil Davidson also sheds light on West African trans-Atlantic exploration. He writes that "Omari, in the tenth chapter of his *Masalik Al-Absar* reproduces a story which suggests that Atlantic voyages were made by mariners of West Africa in the times of Kankan Musa of Mali; and which roundly states that the predecessors of Kankan Musa embarked on the Atlantic with two hundred ships and sailed westward and disappeared."

Omari, an African historian, indicated that he received an account of the voyages from Ibn Amir Hajib, another scholar in Cairo, Egypt who spoke directly to "Sultan Musa." Davidson reproduced the conversation in his book, *The Lost Cities of Africa*:

> And I asked the Sultan Musa how it was that power had come to his hands and he replied: 'We come of a house where royalty is transferred by heritage. The monarch who preceded me would not believe that it was impossible to discover the limits of the neighboring sea. He wished to know. He persisted in his plan. He caused the equipping of two hundred ships and filled them with men, and another such number that were filled with gold, water and food for two years. He said to the commanders: 'do not return until you have reached the end of the ocean, or when you have exhausted your food and water.'
>
> They went away, and their absence was long; none came back, and their

absence continued. Then a single ship returned. We asked its captain of their adventures and their news. He replied: 'Sultan, we sailed for a long while until we met with what seemed to be a river with a strong current flowing in the open sea. My ship was last. The others sailed on, but as each of them came to that place they did not come back, nor did they reappear; and I do not know what became of them. As for me, I turned where I was and did not enter that current.'

The western boundary of the empire of Mali was the Atlantic Ocean. The coast of what now is Senegal and Gambia would have provided several good starting places for such expeditions. North African mariners evidently knew of the Canaries and possibly the Azores several centuries before the voyage of Columbus. Did Africans explore America especially Mexico and Central America before Columbus? Existing evidence would indicate that they could and did.

There is, of course, one final piece of evidence of African presence in America before the time of Columbus. Both Van Sertima and Fell mention it. In 1975 at Hull Bay in the Virgin Islands scientists from the Smithsonian Institution discovered the skeletal remains of two adult African males in soil layers dated to 1250 A.D. The teeth of each thirty year old man had been filed down in a distinctively African fashion. One wore a wristband clearly showing pre-Columbian Indian workmanship. Van Sertima relates that because of salt water damage to the gravesite and the resultant problems with carbon dating, he believes the Smithsonian will soon abandon its discovery.

THE AGE OF COLUMBUS

Columbus' famed voyage of exploration began Europe's first headlong rush to the Americas. And although it is seldom recognized, Africans were involved in the exploits of Columbus.

Some scholars consider noteworthy the fact that Columbus dropped into the more southerly latitudes such as African explorers would have taken. J.A. Rogers, advanced the theory that Columbus had been influenced by Africans that had gone to Spain. Indeed, it is Columbus himself who verifies this statement. Writing to the Spanish sovereigns in 1501, he stated "My intercourse and conversation center around people of wisdom... as well as secular scholars, Latins, Greeks, Indians and Moors."

As a young man in his thirties, Columbus sailed to the Guinea coast of West Africa as part of a Portuguese slaving mission. He is believed to have visited the Portuguese slaving fortress of Sao Jorge da Mina (Elmina) on the shore of the Gold Coast. The sights and sounds he encountered on this voyage further stirred his dreams. Columbus was new to the heat of the tropics with its unfamiliar plants and animals and different wind patterns. This voyage also undeniably impressed him with the efficacy and potential wealth of the slave trade.

About 1490, Martin Pinzon who commanded a ship on Columbus' first voyage, told him of finding an account in the Vatican library of the Queen of Sheba's transatlantic crossing to Japan. This also inspired Columbus. Although no trace of this document has since been found, even Samuel Elliot Morrison in his most famous book on Columbus did not entirely dismiss the existence of such a document.

Columbus, in his journal also made reference to Negro traders from Guinea who trafficked in a gold alloy "guanin" of precisely the same composition and bearing the same name as frequently referred to as early writers in Africa. H.G. Lawrence amplified this in his *Crisis* article:

> Columbus was informed by some men, when he stopped at the Cape Verde Islands off the coast of Africa, that Negroes had been known to set out in the Atlantic from the Guinea Coast in canoes loaded with merchandise and steering toward the west... Columbus was further informed by the Indians of Hispaniola when he arrived in the West Indies that they had been unable to obtain gold from black men who had come from across the sea from the south and the southeast... It must also be added that Amerigo Vespucci on his voyage to the Americas witnessed these same black men out in the Atlantic returning to Africa.

Evidence suggests that at least one crewman on Columbus' first voyage was possibly black. Pedro Alonso Nino of the ship Nina is thought to have been black by some historians. There is also some evidence to indicate that Alonzo Pietro, the pilot of the flagship Santa Maria may have been black. While the debate contunues on the racial identity of Nino and Pietro, there is firmer evidence about another African companion of Columbus.

On Columbus' fourth and last voyage which set sail in July 1502, a crewman of the caravel "Capitana" is called "Diego el Negro." He was one of twenty gromets or ship's boys on Columbus' 70-ton flagship. His job was to wait upon the ship's senior officers and passengers. Diego el Negro was paid 666 maravedis a month, a small but standard wage for that type of shipboard occupation. Like the other ship's boys, he would have been under the age of seventeen.

Diego el Negro was part of Columbus' total force of four ships and 150 men that explored the coastline of Central America stopping in Honduras, Costa Rica, and Panama. He is also believed to have been with Columbus when he was temporarily stranded in Jamaica. Other blacks may have sailed with Columbus on his second and third voyages but complete crew lists for those expeditions have not yet been located.

Although tiny Portugal established the first overseas empire, Spain, its larger, stronger, and more populous neighbor overtook it in the race for possessions in the New World. With the exception of Brazil, Portugal turned toward the east developing trade and colonies in the Orient. Spain sent its ships and men to California and the Chesapeake Bay, around the world with Magellan, and from Nova Scotia to Peru.

After 1500 A.D. increasing numbers of blacks accompanied Spanish expeditions to North, Central and South America; the territory called "New Spain." They came to the new lands as slaves or freed men from Spain. By 1450 Portuguese slave ships were disembarking hundreds of native Africans each year into western Europe, particularly Portugal and Spain. This area already had a significant mixture of black blood because of the long Moorish occupation. Over 35,000 African slaves lived in Portugal by 1492.

Lisbon and Seville were among the major cities on the Iberian Peninsula with large black populations. Some of these blacks or their children became Hispanized or thoroughly acculturated. They became prime movers in the subjugation of Native American culture and the expansion of European colonialism. Other blacks left their Hispanic masters as soon as they arrived in America and allied themselves with Native Americans in the cause of freedom.

In Brazil, because of Portugal's virtual monopoly of the African slave trade, the majority of its black residents came directly from the African slave coast. When the available supply of blacks from Europe was used up, the brutality of slavery had nearly extinguished local Native Americans, and white settlers showed themselves disinclined toward heavy labor, slave imports directly from Africa skyrocketed. By 1810 a million African slaves toiled in Portuguese and Spanish America.

Strong African hands and backs were needed to mine the gold, iron and copper on the islands and mainland, plant and harvest sugar cane introduced by Columbus in 1493 and eventually more lucrative than the anemic gold deposits of the West Indies, and to serve as porters, soldiers, teamsters, farmers, servants, craftsmen, and mechanics.

In 1513, Vasco Nunez de Balboa had thirty blacks (including one named Nuflo de Olano) with him when he discovered the Pacific Ocean. Also with him were over one hundred Spaniards and at least two hundred Indians. During the forced march through dense jungle and terrible swamps, Balboa and his men came upon an Indian village. To his surprise, he was shown two black prisoners of war. The Indians were unable to tell where these blacks had come from except to say that they lived nearby and often fought the local Indians. Balboa believed that these men were black Spanish slaves or freedmen. They were Africans and the first he had seen already "in the Indies."

Peter Martyr, a contemporary historian, wrote of this strange meeting, that the "... Negroes in this province... live only one day's march from Quarequa and they are fierce ... It is thought that Negro pirates from Ethiopia established themselves after the wreck of their ships in these mountains. The natives of Quarequa carry on incessant war with these Negroes. Massacre or slavery is the alternative future of these people."

Also in 1513, Ponce de Leon, who had already forcibly subdued the natives of Puerto Rico, sailed from there to a peninsula he called Pascua Florida. Some historians believe that one of his companions on this first recorded trip to Florida was a mulatto named Pedro Mexia. He married Donna Lusia, an Indian female and was killed protecting her from members of her tribe angry over her conversion to Catholicism.

In 1519, Hernando Cortes set out to explore and conquer Mexico. Approximately 200 Africans took part in this expedition as they helped to drag his large cannon.

Bernal Diaz del Castillo, who accompanied Cortes and was the author of *The Discovery and Conquest of Mexico*, mentions several Africans. Juan Sedeno was one of the richest soldiers in the eleven-ship fleet that invaded Mexico. Of Sedeno, Diaz tells us that "he came in his own ship with a mare, and a Negro." Diaz adds that "at that time horses and Negroes were worth their weight in gold and that is the reason why more horses were not taken, for there were none to be bought." Negroes, however, were plentiful, so I think it possible that blacks outnumbered the sixteen horses brought along on the voyage.

Diego Velasquez, an administrator for the Spanish Crown and financier for the Cortes expedition, later became jealous and distrustful of the wealth and fame that Cortes was garnering and sent an expedition (Diaz says 19 ships) to capture him in Mexico. This unsuccessful expedition was commanded by Panfilo de Narvaez and included two blacks.

As the time of battle grew closer, Cortes' lieutenants sent out a reconnaissance patrol. Of the two-man patrol Diaz says "they were dark complexioned men; they did not look like Spaniards." These men were probably Spanish Moors or their descendants with still visible traces of African blood. The intelligence mission was successful, the two spies ended their brief sojourn in the enemy camp by stealing the saddle, bridle and horse of one of Cortes' arch enemies and using this animal to make a hurried exit from their foe's camp.

About three days later, the battle took place and men were killed and wounded on both sides (Narvaez lost an eye and was imprisoned by Cortes). With presents of gold and jewels, Cortes bought the allegiance of the surviving members of the Narvaez punitive expedition. Among those brought to Cortes' side by promises of wealth was Guidela, a black soldier-drummer whom Diaz describes as "a very witty jester." Diaz also states that a black man whom Narvaez brought with him introduced smallpox into Mexico and that a large number of Indians died because they had no resistance to the disease.

Smallpox, a deadly and contagious virus, was a disease with which Europeans and Africans had familiarity and respect. Because of repeated exposure many of them had become virtually immune to the high fever, skin eruptions and other ravages of the disease. The native peoples of the Americas, living on another continent primarily in small groups had developed no such resistance. Smallpox erupted though their ranks killing millions.

It is not clear to what extent this black soldier is responsible for the smallpox outbreak.

Figure 30

The colonization of Latin America

The disease first appeared in the Americas in 1519 on the island of Santo Domingo. Within four years, it was reported in Peru. Geoffrey Crowley's article in the Fall/Winter 1991 issue of *Newsweek* magazine describes the nature of the disease: "The disaster began almost as soon as Columbus arrived, fueled mainly by smallpox and measles... Outbreaks spread across the Antilles, onto the Mexican mainland, through the Isthmus of Panama and into South America. The Spaniards were moving in the same direction, but their diseases often outpaced them." Crowley quoted Alfred Crosby, author of *The Columbian Exchange*: "Such is the communicability of smallpox and other eruptive fevers that any Indians who received news of the Spaniards could also have easily received the infection."

Another chronicler of the Cortes expedition, Jose Antonio Saco, tells us that a black man named Juan Carrido, near the end of the Mexican conquest in 1521 planted the first wheat crop in the Americas. Carrido had brought the grains of wheat in his haversack from Spain. He planted the crop as an experiment and as such became an agricultural pioneer in the annals of American history.

It was regular Spanish custom to divide the loot taken in battle. A "royal fifth" was set aside for the Spanish crown. Then the rest was divided among the soldiers. Mounted troops got twice what infantrymen received. Officers collected according to grade. These were incentives for many blacks to fight for Spain.

In the summer of 1526 the Spanish crown gave Lucas Vasquez de Allyon permission to establish a colony in the New World. With 500 Spanish colonists, 100 African slaves, three priests, and several horses, de Allyon set sail in six ships from the island of Hispaniola. Bound for Florida, he wrecked one ship, and landed near the mouth of the Pee Dee River near Cape Fear in North Carolina.

De Allyon chose a swampy spot of land for the colony he called "San Miguel." The African slaves performed the heavy labor. They cleared land, erected houses for the colonists and started a fort. The Spanish, more concerned with finding gold, pressed the Indians to lead then to the riches. The Native Americans began to desert. Sickness overtook the Spaniards. Allyon died of fever in October. The Africans planned a revolt aided by the Indians. Bickering erupted among the Spaniards as dozens of the colonists died. By late November, the Africans had revolted and fled to safety and freedom among the local Native Americans.

The 150 Spaniards who remained in San Miguel decided to return to Hispaniola. This ended the first foreign colony established in what is now the United States.

In 1527, a five hundred man expedition under the command of Panfilo de Narvaez, the old enemy of Cortes, left Spain to explore the northern and western shores of the Gulf of Mexico. His five ships were blown off course and landed far to the east of their objective, the Sarasota-Tampa Bay region of what is now Florida. They were somewhere in a land called Texas.

It had not been a good voyage. Over a hundred men had jumped ship and 70 others lost their lives in a storm at sea. Narvaez split his force taking most of the remaining men with him overland. The rest of the men were ordered back into the boats to sail along the coastline. Both groups would meet later according to Narvaez's plans.

Steadily moving west by land and boat the participants in this ill-starred adventure were racked by desertions, starvation, cannibalism, an unhealthy climate, and hostile Indians. They were reduced in number from eighty (including de Narvaez) to fifteen to four. These four men, Cabeza de Vaca, the treasurer of the expedition; Alonzo de Castillo, Andres Dorantes, and his Moroccan-born black slave Estevanico (Esteban) were to suffer incredible hardships as Indian slaves for six years. The three whites and one black slowly ingratiated themselves with their masters and over the long years devised a plan of escape. In September 1534, it was successful. Their destination was Mexico City far to the southwest.

For another two years they wandered over the countryside posing as medicine men, with Estevanico who had developed a kind of rapport with the Indians, often leading the way. Of this time Cabeza de Vaca would later write in his *Narrative*, "The Negro was in constant conversation. He informed himself about the ways we wish to take, of the towns there, and the matters we desired to know." At the end of the arduous journey, Estevanico who could neither read nor write, spoke at least five of the varying Indian languages of those regions and was a master of the silent art of sign language. These self made medicine men attracted a large following of Native Americans on their trip.

De Vaca described how the party knew they were getting closer to civilization; the burned remains of an Indian village put to the torch by a caravan of Spanish slavers and distrustful Indians angered by the ruthlessness of Spanish military expeditions.

Of their rescue, de Vaca wrote that he "came upon Christians on horseback, who received a great shock to see me, so strangely dressed and accompanied by Indians...I told them to bring me to where their captain was...and I asked him to give me a certificate of the year and the month and the day in which I had arrived there and the manner in which I came, and thus it was done."

In 1536, some eight years after the Narvaez expedition had touched the verdant shores of Texas, the four survivors entered Mexico City. De Vaca, Castillo and Dorantes (after having sold Estevanico to Antonio Mendoza, the viceroy of New Spain and the successor to Cortes) promptly returned to Old Spain. Before they separated the four men had excited all the government officials with the wild tales the Indians had given them of the seven golden cities of Cibola somewhere to the northwest.

Mendoza organized an exploration party headed by Fray Marcos de Niza, a Franciscan monk, to search for these cities. The group also included Fray Onoruto, and a lay brother. Estevanico was the guide. His independent spirit grown restless after his two years of virtual freedom, Estevanico, realized his importance to the expedition and perhaps inwardly made a vow to be slave in mind (if not in body) no longer.

In March, 1539, after a final briefing from Mendoza, Estevanico, de Niza, and the others departed their base at San Miguel in Mexico and began their walk into history.

Estevanico decided to play the role of god, medicine man and explorer to the hilt. The African forged ahead of the group accompanied by a retinue of Indians, a dinner service of colored plates, two greyhounds, and a gourd rattle decorated with feathers. The rattle had been given to him as a symbol of authority and power by other Indians during his travels with Cabeza de Vaca.

The initial part of the journey took Estevanico back into familiar territory. He had come this way years earlier on his way to Mexico City with his three white comrades. The path they took passed through a tiny hamlet called Petatlan and then onto a larger village called Vacapa, near the northernmost border of the present state of Sinaloa.

The group had by this time been on the trail about two weeks and it was here that de Niza sent the black man still farther ahead of the group. De Niza wrote in his account of the expedition, "I sent Estevan Dorantes the Negro another way, whom I commanded to go directly northward for fifty of threescore leagues, to see if by that way he might learn news of any notable thing which we sought."

Estevanico could not write so in order to communicate the black man reported his observations to de Niza by Indian couriers bearing crosses. "That is it were but a mean thing" de Niza instructed, "he would send me a white cross of one handful long; and if it were any great matter, one of two handfuls long; and if it were a country greater and better than Nueva Espana, he should send me a great crosse."

On Easter Sunday with a bevy of Indian females and his other Indian companions Estevanico left camp. Four days later, Indian runners brought de Niza "a great crosse as high as a man." We can no longer accurately tell exactly what happened to the African from this point on — Estevanico would be killed several weeks after he left camp, what follows is based on the accounts of de Niza, Coronado, and Castaneda (another member of the group).

Estevanico continually queried the Indians about the cities of Cibola. Roughly 30 days journey from Estevanico, the Indians told de Niza was a "very mighty Province." North, go north, the neighboring Indians told de Niza, north to a land of seven rich cities all under the rule of one lord. The monk did as he was told and followed in the wake of Estevanico.

At this point, according to his instructions and since he was on the verge (supposedly) of reaching Cibola the African was to wait until de Niza and the rest of the party caught up with him. Estevanico's precise reasons for disobeying the friar's command are unknown. But for whatever reason, gold, glory, or something else, Estevanico increased his rate of travel and rushed to his death.

He dressed himself with shining metal bells and colored plumes and performed feats of magic in front of the Indians to convince them he had divine authority. He passed through the Sonora Valley, pushed across the San Pedro River and into what is now Arizona. Estevanico reached the Arivaipa Valley, the Pinaleno and Santa Teresa mountain ranges and then turned northward to the Gila River. It was from here that he conveyed his final message to the priest.

The black explorer moved northward until his Indian guides told him he was but one day from Cibola. Estevancio was now near the modern site of St. Johns, Arizona. He dressed himself as splendidly as possible, sent out runners to announce his coming and gave them his decorated gourd as a sign of authority and friendship.

Early the next day, his Indian companions returned fearful and distraught. The Lord of Cibola had smashed Estevanico's gourd and he further commanded Estevanico to turn back or he and his party would suffer death. (It has been suggested that the chief of the

Cibolans recognized the decorations on the gourd as belonging to a tribe hostile to the Cibolans).

Estevanico, spurred by his successes with the other tribes he had encountered, paid no heed to the warnings. It was the first week of May 1539.

Estevanico and his entourage of 300 Indians were halted near the main entrance to the town. The Cibolans were suspicious and remained utterly unconvinced once they heard the African's story of being an emissary for a people with white skins who were sent by a great lord in the sky.

For approximately two days the Cibolans discussed the matter. The Cibolans decided to kill him in an effort to keep the location of their village hidden from the Spaniards. He was shot with arrows and the skin cut from his body; proof positive to the Indians that he was no god.

The Lord of Cibola kept Estevanico's greyhounds, bright dinner crockery, and all the treasures the African had brought with him. This was the gist of what the Indian survivors of the massacre at Cibola told de Niza. The friar claimed that after this he journeyed to a hill overlooking Cibola. He told Mendoza that he had seen a very beautiful town with stone houses and that it appeared to him to be larger in size than Mexico City.

Estevanico (Little Stephen), sometimes called "Esteban," was the first non-Indian to explore parts of Texas, New Mexico, and Arizona. His daring exploits, skill and incredible hardiness live on in the folklore of the Zuni Indians of New Mexico as recorded by the black scholar Monroe Work in the 1925 *Negro Yearbook*.

> "When the roofs lay over the walls of Kyakime, when the smoke hung over the housetops,then the Mexicans came from their abodes in the ever-lasting summerland. These Indians So-no-li, set up a great howl and thus they and our ancients did much ill to one another. Then and thus was killed by our ancients right where the stone stands down by the arroyo of Kyakime one of the black Mexicans, a large man with chili lips...then the rest ran away, chased by our grandfathers, and went back toward their own country in the land of the everlasting summer."

On the basis of de Nizas' information, the viceroy authorized another expedition in search of Cibola. This was led by Francisco Vasquez de Coronado, the governor of New Galicia and a protege of the viceroy. The stories and legends surrounding Estevanico also acted as an impetus for the exploration of Hernando de Soto.

Coronado started out in 1540. A contemporary described the expedition as having "three hundred horsemen, two hundred foot soldiers, all splendidly, even gorgeously attired and accoutered...one of them was Coronado, wearing a suit of golden armor." Indians and several blacks also went along to work about the camp and care for livestock.

Delilah L. Beasley, the author of *The Negro Trail Blazers of California*, had the original Spanish records translated. She wrote that "Governor Coronado" had several blacks and even a "Negro Priest" in his expedition.

Coronado and his men explored the mountains and plains of Arizona, New Mexico, Texas, Colorado, Oklahoma and Kansas, some 3,000 miles of territory.

Blacks also sailed with Alarcon, as he supported the Coronado expedition with ship-

Figure 31

DeSoto's discovery of the Mississippi

borne supplies. By land and sea, Coronado's men searched for the elusive wealth of the land and its original inhabitants. And as Coronado crossed the plains of Texas and Oklahoma, de Soto's men were moving through the forests of that same region. Several times the two expeditions were not far apart and the indigenous Indians told them of each other's presence.

Coronado found that there was no golden Cibola, just a group of not stone but mud pueblos inhabited by the Hawikuh, ancestors of the Zuni Indians. The anxious members of the desert excursion sadly shook their heads and cursed when they realized that they had sought to find gold and jewels that had never existed.

How ironic it was when the conquistadors found only a set of colored dishes and two greyhounds; all that remained of Estevanico.

In 1542 Coronado and the bedraggled survivors of his party returned to Mexico dispirited and sorely tried by their fruitless searching. They were the first outsiders to see the Grand Canyon and to describe the Pueblo Indians but such was the hunger of the Spanish authorities for gold these accomplishments meant little. For his conduct of the expedition, Coronado underwent an official inspection and was initially indicted but declared innocent in 1551. Four years later he died. De Niza, his guide, was ruined. He died in disgrace in 1558.

In southern Arizona, near the Sierra Vista Pass through the Huachuca mountains, is the Coronado National Memorial in honor of the Spanish explorer and Estevanico who had gone through the pass a year earlier. In the neighboring state of New Mexico the ruins of the Hawikuh Pueblo where Estevanico was killed still stand.

While Coronado was seeking gold on the plains and deserts of the Midwest and West, Hernando de Soto forged a bloody path across much of what is now the southeastern United States. In 1539 he personally financed an expedition of over 600 men (including four blacks), seven ships, and 300 horses. He was in search of gold. His orders from the King were to "conquer and populate."

In May he landed at Tampa Bay on "Tierra Florida," the land of flowers. Before the end of summer he had fought several battles with the Indians, often killing them without warning.

De Soto even made hostages of friendly Indians. This tactic led to a major battle with four hundred Indians in northern Florida. His men killed or enslaved most of the defeated Native Americans. The winter of 1539-1540 nearly exhausted the supplies of de Soto's men. Battles with Indians sapped the strength of the soldiers and horses. But early in the spring of 1540 de Soto and his men heard stories of a wealthy Indian queen living far inland. Somewhere in northern Georgia they crossed into the land of Cofitachequi.

The Queen of Cofitachequi turned out to be only a princess. Instead of gold they found large pieces of polished copper. Instead of silver there was only sparkling mica. The only things the tiny heiress had in abundance were fresh water pearls, still available in many parts of the South today. De Soto had his men gather 350 pounds of pearls and march on. One of the Africans remained behind, married the princess of the pearls; and became the prince of Cofitachequi, at least this is the story the expedition's survivors told when they returned.

Figure 32

Plantation life — Brazil

Figure 33

Gathering cane

The truth may be a bit more ordinary. De Soto's force crossed into Alabama just west of Rome, Georgia. On July 26, 1540, they saw a large Indian village on a hill high above acres of planted crops and a forest teeming with game. This was a city of Coosa, which is now Childersburg, Alabama in Talladega County. Chief Coosa greeted the Spaniards with open palms, a sign of friendship. His people sang and danced in front of the strangers. The Native Americans reserved their greatest curiosity for the Spaniards' horses. They had never seen such beasts.

Despite such a welcome, de Soto made captives of Chief Coosa and his nobles. He did this to force the Indians to give him food and slaves. The Spaniards stayed in Coosa about a month. They left behind a soldier named Furado and one ill black man. These two men are believed to be the first non-Indians to make a permanent home in the New World.

A federal government study, *Final Report of the De Soto Expedition Commission*, confirms the historical importance of Coosa. The presence of these two settlers is nearly a century before the pilgrims came to Massachusetts, seven decades before the English landed at Jamestown in Virginia, and is twenty-five years earlier than Pedro Menendez de Aviles' founding of St. Augustine, Florida in 1565, generally regarded as the first permanent European settlement in what is now the United States. Black slave labor erected the walls of the fort of Ft. Augustine and many of that city's earliest buildings.

The high point of the de Soto expedition was their discovery of the Mississippi River in 1541. On a Sunday in early May, the Spaniards stuggled through underbrush and stopped at the banks of the largest river they had seen since they had landed fourteen months earlier. They called it the "Rio Grande" and estimated the far bank was at least two miles away. They were just south of what is now Memphis, Tennessee. De Soto had heard many stories about such a great river. After allowing his men to eat and rest, de Soto ordered them to build barges and rafts to cross the river. Within a month they had moved on. It remained for others to discover the true importance of the river the Indians called the "Father of Waters."

The following year de Soto died of fever. He was succeeded by Luis Moscoso. He led the three hundred surviving Spaniards back to Mexico in 1543. De Soto's men had traveled nearly 4,000 miles but they never found the gold they so eagerly sought.

De Soto had first won the fortune he later squandered on the Mississippi when he served with Francisco Pizarro and his partner Amalgro during the plunder and destruction of the Inca empire in Peru. Africans played a variety of roles in the early European encounter with the Mayas, Incas, and Muiscas. Pizarro also helped found the Panama City. He also founded Lima, Peru.

Pizarro requested permission from the Spanish Crown to bring in fifty blacks before he invaded Peru. One of these Africans was named Bombon, according to J.A. Rogers. Another was second in command of Pizarro's artillery during the Battle of Cajamarca on November 16, 1532. The Spanish trapped thousands of Incas in the plaza of the city and slaughtered them. Atahualpa, the "sapa Inca" or king was captured. It was here that he made his famous offer to ransom himself by filling a large room with gold and another twice over with silver.

The Incas virtually kept their word. They delivered 11 tons of wrought gold objects and

26,000 pounds of silver. Pizarro's share was 630 pounds of gold and 1200 pounds of silver. But it did not him keep from killing Atahualpa. He was choked to death in July 1535.

Pizarro was assassinated in 1541 by a dissident group of Spaniards led by the son of his former partner, Amalgro. Blacks carried Pizzaro's body to the cathedral in Lima.

Two hundred blacks marched with Pedro de Alvarado when he trekked to the northern fringes of the Inca empire in Ecuador. Many of them died of frost bite. Ortal, Sedeno, and Heredia each brought 100 black slaves to exploit the forests of Venezuela.

Juan Valiente, a fugitive black slave from Mexico, found wealth serving with the Spanish explorers in South America. He sailed with Diego de Amalgro to explore Chile, along with 150 other Africans.

On the pampas of Chile, he fought beside Pedro de Valdivia who also had several blacks with him. De Valdivia, established the city of Santiago, Chile in 1539. Near this city, Valiente settled and became an "ecomendero." He employed Indian labor and was obligated to teach them the Christian religion and protect them from ill treatment. He married Juana Valdivia who may have been related to his Spanish comrade-in-arms.

In New Mexico, Sebastian Rodriguez Brito, (a free black) was the drummer of the Santa Fe garrison. The records of the Archdiocese of Santa Fe first make mention of him on May 29, 1689, when he filed a marriage petition. In his petition Brito described himself as "de nacion angola."

Brito was born in Portuguese Guinea in 1642 of parents described as "Negros bosales" or jungle Negroes. He saw service (probably as a drummer) with Governor Pasada in 1686 and beginning in 1691 with Governor Don Diego de Vargas. As well as being a drummer, Brito was also the town crier or governor's herald.

That Brito actually performed this additional function is attested to in a book describing Governor de Vargas' decision to lead an expedition into New Mexico to recover lands lost to the Native Americans. The August 1692 military incursion "was publicly announced to the sound of the war drum and bugle... in the most public places, loudly and intelligibly by the voice of Sebastian Rodriguez...," according to historian J.M. Espinosa. Brito also served in de Vargas' second expedition as well.

Through a score of heated engagements with the Indians, Brito served coolly and steadily under fire. Brito also owned land on the south side of the Santa Fe River in New Mexico.

About the same time (c. 1692) another free black, Jose Lopez Naranjo was appointed a Major War-Captain of Indian auxiliary troops. This position and title was later handed down through two generations of the same family. In Texas, about 1691, a black bugler was one of Domingo Teran's soldiers on the second Spanish missionary expedition. The objective of the Spaniards was to convert the Indians of East Texas to the Catholic faith.

In 1769, the Spaniard Gaspar de Portola, with Father Junipero Serra, explored upper (alta) California. He camped at what is now San Diego, rode to Monterey Bay, and skirted the edge of San Francisco Bay. His men called it "the great arm of the sea." Juan Antonio Coronel served as a foot soldier on this expedition. There were also a handful of black teamsters on this journey.

When Juan Bautista de Anza established a supply route from Sonora in Mexico to the

Spanish missions in California in 1775, seven black soldiers served in his 30-man force. The following year de Anza established an outpost that later became the city of San Francisco.

Black and Indian slaves were the twin pillars that supported the Spanish regime in the New World. Somewhat like the use of fire, the presence of black slaves proved simultaneously desirable yet dangerous.

From the first years of their introduction into the colonies blacks along with Indians rebelled against their Spanish masters. For example when a royal decree in 1501 provided for the first direct importation of African slaves into Hispaniola, many Spaniards were divided over the issue because of the possible rebelliousness of African slaves.

In 1503, the governor of Hispaniola angrily wrote to the King of Spain that his African slaves "fled among the Indians and taught them bad customs and never would be captured." Nineteen years later the same situation still persisted, in that year Diego Columbus, brother of Christopher, personally took part in the suppression of a slave revolt on Hispaniola in 1522. The next year the governor of Mexico ordered an embargo on black slaves because of conflicts in that colony. Slave revolts took place in Mexico in 1537, 1669, and 1735. Revolts also occurred in Panama, Columbia, Honduras, Puerto Rico, and Cuba. In 1521, Spain briefly considered banning Africans from accompanying expeditions because so many ran away to join the Indians.

An outstanding example of African and Native American cooperation against the Spanish is the Pueblo Revolt of 1680.

On an August day in 1680 twenty one monks and several families were killed. As a result of the attacks by the Indians, Spanish forces were rolled back to the southern mission center of Guadelupe del Paso (Cuidad Juarez, Mexico). The conflict, although primarily religious in nature, was instigated by a black man who claimed to be a lieutenant of their Indian god Po-he-yemu. Governor Otermin in the journal he kept for 1681 reported that this lieutenant of Po-he-yemu was "very tall, black, and had very large yellow eyes" and everyone feared him greatly. It has since been determined that his name may have been Naranjo.

The Indian, El Pope of San Juan along with Naranjo welded the dissident pueblos for a short time into an effective fighting force by uniting religious zeal with effective tactics. In the end, however, they were overwhelmed by the power of Spain.

Blacks on an individual basis continually tried to subvert, thwart or kill the Europeans in front of their Indian allies. The killing of the friar de Acenedo in Sinaloa in 1561 is attributed to a mulatto interpreter who purposely twisted his words.

Blacks often escaped from Spanish exploring parties and joined the Indians or were left behind by the explorers. Black members of the Coronado, De Soto, and de Allyon expeditions lived with Native Americans. The Leyva de Bonilla-Umana party left a black woman with Kansas Indians in the 1590's.

Decades earlier blacks had joined Indians in the mountainous recesses of nearly every island in the West Indies and in South America. Here they formed maroon communities to fight European domination. In *Black Indians*, William L. Katz describes two female leaders of the resistance communities. One of them, "Filippa Maria Amanda, an African,

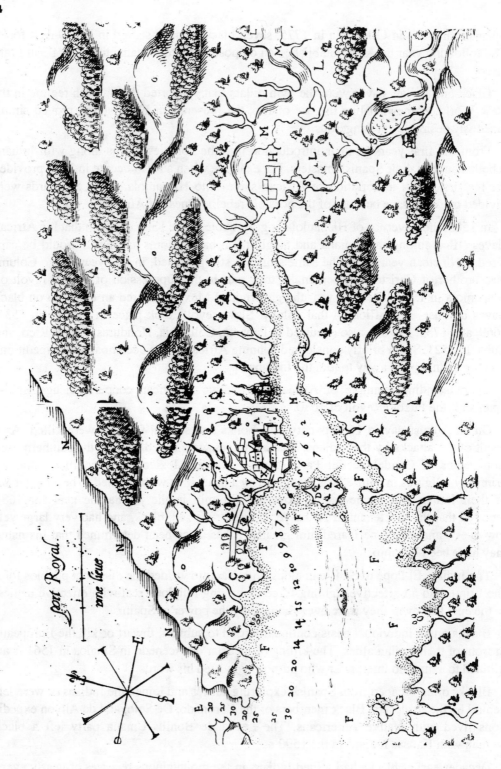

Figure 34

Samuel de Champlain's map of Port Royal in Nova Scotia, Canada

ruled a thriving colony in Amazonia, Brazil." This country was also home to the Republic of Palmares, a nation of maroons established in 1645. The first independent African political state in the western hemisphere existed until 1697. Palmares fell after repulsing twenty-six assaults by the Dutch and Portuguese.

The late 1500s and early 1600s saw other European powers nibbling at the edges of Spain's vast territory in the New World. This empire had been born out of blood, greed, ruthlessness, cunning, spirit, and even luck for the Spaniards. For the majority of Africans, the New World was an unwelcome shore where slavery and degradation threatened to break the body and cripple the soul. To the Native Americans, it was the time when the world was spoiled. Uncomprehending cultures collided. Millions of Indians were extinguished for a trinity of forces: gold, God and glory. Oviedo, the Spanish historian tells us that men from every corner of the globe took part in the excesses that forged the New World, "from all the other nations of Asia, Africa and Europe."

France and England, even tiny Holland and Sweden, sent out men and ships probing, contesting Spain's power. Later they fought each other for the remnants of Spain's North American empire. France was the only other European power to significantly involve blacks in its explorations. The other European nations employed black laborers and craftsmen, both slave and free, in their early settlements.

Blacks were with the French pioneers and Jesuit missionaries in Canada and along the Mississippi River. The earliest black explorer in Canada (then called New France) was Mathieu da Costa. He was an interpreter who spoke Micmac, the Alonquian language and name for a large Indian tribe inhabiting the Maritime Provinces and Newfoundland. Da Costa was a slave of Pierre du Gua, Sieur de Monts, one of Samuel de Champlains' chief partners. Described as "a well-educated and Baptized Negro," da Costa had arrived in Canada, spent time among the Micmacs, left the country and later returned to assist the French. Da Costa died during the winter of 1606-1607 at Port Royal in Nova Scotia, one of the towns founded by Champlain.

In 1564 French Protestants settled in what became Jacksonville, Florida among their number were several Africans. In the expedition led by Pere Marquette, a priest, and Louis Joliet, a fur trader, at least one African took part, as early as 1673. They paddled down the Mississippi to its junction with the Arkansas River extending French influence into the Midwest. The French Jesuit colony built in 1736 at Fort Kaskaskia (near Chester, Illinois) included seventy blacks.

The founder of Chicago was a black trader, Jean Baptiste Pointe Du Sable in 1779. After a career as an explorer in the midwest and trader on the southern shore of Lake Michigan (c. 1772), Du Sable built a trading post in a marshland called by the Indians "Es-ch-ka-gou" or stinking onions. Busy and prosperous, Du Sable provided all the services a frontier settlement needed. He sold flour, pork, beef, salt, cloth, milk and bread. On his premises were a livery stable, mill, and a cooperage.

Du Sable is believed to have been born in St. Marc, Saint-Dominque (Haiti) around 1745. An English officer, Colonel de Peyster, described meeting Du Sable in the summer of 1779. "Baptist (sic) Point de Sable, a handsome Negro, well educated and settled at Eschihagou but was much in the interest of the French."

British forces were keenly aware of French designs on the area. Between 1689 and

1763, they fought four separate wars with each other over the control of eastern Canada, Nova Scotia, and what is now New England. The Treaty of Paris in 1763 was to have ended France's power in the region. British forces were still keeping a tense vigil in 1779.

De Peyster arrested Du Sable twice. Each time he was charged with "treasonable intercourse with the enemy." There was little evidence to convict him. He was released and ordered out of the immediate area. In 1784, Du Sable went back to Chicago. He stayed until 1800 selling his trading post and outbuildings for over a thousand dollars.

By 1805 his wanderlust had taken him to St. Charles, Missouri. Here he deeded some land and a house to his granddaughter, Eulalie Derais. Du Sable had married Catherine, a Potawatomi Indian in 1788. The couple had three children, Suzanne, John Baptiste, Jr., and Catherine.

Du Sable died in St. Charles, Missouri in 1818. He is buried in St. Charles Borromeo Cemetery. In Chicago today, there are several memorials to Du Sable. These include a high school named in his honor and a famous black history museum.

At St. Genevieve, a small French town down river from St. Louis, Missouri, black slaves were among its earliest inhabitants. In the center of a stretch of rich bottom land, the town also had a mine and a salt lick. Of its 676 settlers in 1773, St. Genevieve counted 276 African slaves.

Blacks were also among early Dutch inhabitants on Manhattan Island just a few years after Peter Minuit bought the land from Native Americans for $24.00 worth of trinkets and glass beads. A black named Francisko was one of the founders of the town of Bushwick in what is now Brooklyn, New York.

In the late 1700's blacks accompanied English settlers into what is now Minnesota. One such black family gave rise to two generations of Afro-Indian explorers and fur traders. The family name was Bonga. Beginning with Pierre and later his sons, George and Stephen, the Bongas' explored northern Minnesota, caught beavers, and lived with and later married Chippewa Indians. George represented the Chippewa at the 1837 treaty negotiations in the United States. The Bonga township in Cass County is named for them.

Blacks came to the English colonies first as slaves in 1619. Free blacks from Barbados, however, were among the first explorers and settlers of Maryland. Mathias de Sousa, Francisco Peres, and John Price served as pilots on the "Ark" and the "Dove," the English ships. They guided the small fragile ships through the Atlantic from the West Indies to St. Clements' Island in the Chesapeake Bay. A few days later the party went ashore on the mainland and established St. Mary's County, the oldest in Maryland. The blacks went on to become leading members of the community.

A multi-national contingent of settlers (including blacks, Spanish, and French) under the leadership of Antonio Gil Ygarbo, after a series of misfortunes, founded one of the oldest and most important towns of east Texas, Nacogdoches, in 1779.

In 1781, Los Angeles, California was founded by forty-four persons (11 families) of whom 16 were Indian, 26 were black and two were white. The first official resident (by virtue of being the first to volunteer to settle in the area) was a black man, a native of Mexico named Antonio Mesa. (Because of miscegenation and intermarriage, Africans frequently acquired Spanish names.) Maria Rita Valdez, whose black grandparents were among the founding members of Los Angeles, owned Rancho Rodeo de Las Aguas, today known as Beverly Hills. Francisco Reyes, another black resident owned the San Fernando Valley. In the 1790's he sold it and became mayor of Los Angeles.

A Spanish census of 1790 identified 18% of the California population as being of African descent. In a community founded in 1776 called San Jose, the percentage of blacks was 24.3. The capital of alta California, Monterey, supported a population of which 18.5% were of African ancestry. In the area around the settlement of Yerba Buena (what is now San Francisco, California) the percentage was 14.7.

Undoubtedly, the most famous early black family of San Francisco was headed by Santiago Pico. Pico was a mestizo, and his wife was black. Their sons, Jose Dolores, Jose Maria, Miguel, Francisco and Patricio became landowners and soldiers. A grandson, Pio Pico was the last governor of California under Mexican rule (1845-1846). Subsequently, another Pico, Andreas, would assist in leading the resistance to United States annexation in 1846 and 1847.

The young United States pushed relentlessly westward and black explorers were often in the vanguard. After the American Revolution pioneers moved from the East Coast across the Appalachians. Du Sable still lived in the lands that the British ceded to the Americans after the treaty ended the revolution.

When Napoleon, who had received the Louisiana Territory by secret treaty from Spain, sold it to the United States, the black man York helped explore its vastness. The United States doubled in size through this acquisition. The purchase covered land stretching from New Orleans in the South to what is now Montana in the West.

In 1806, the year York and the rest of the Lewis and Clark expedition ended their journey in St. Louis, Edward Rose, another black explorer went west. He joined a group of fur-trappers headed by Manuel Lisa. On barges, Rose, Lisa, and the rest floated into Montana.

After weeks on the water, they beached the barges near the Big Horn River. Here they built a log stockade they called Fort Manuel. They trapped and skinned beaver, hunted and fished, and traded with the local Indian tribes. Rose gained invaluable experience here as a "mountain man." He excelled particularly with Native Americans. They found him eager to learn their languages and cultures, to know the forest, rivers, and sky as they knew them.

Around 1809, he trapped and traded with "Zeke" Williams, returning with him to Montana. Two years later, Rose served as scout and interpreter for Wilson B. Hunt, who took a large group of trappers to the border of the Oregon Territory. Time after time, Rose served as a guide and interpreter for whites moving west.

A big tough bear of a man, Rose had a reputation for bravery and resourcefulness and he knew the frontier and Indians. He spoke nearly a dozen Indian languages. They named him Cut-Nose because of two knife scars on his face. The Crow Indians made him a chief.

Katz quotes Reuben Holmes, the author of the 1848 book, *Five Scalps*, as describing Rose as "...cunning as a prairie wolf... a perfect woodsman. He could endure any kind of fatigue and privation as well as the best trained Indians. He studied men. There was nothing that an Indian could do that Rose did not make himself master of. He knew all that Indians knew. He was a great man in his situation.''

For twenty years Rose continued to add to his fame as a ''voyaguer.'' He and two other men were trapping near the Yellowstone River when the end came in the early 1830's. John Sanford, a local Indian agent, described the event in a letter to General William Clarke:

> The Aricaras have abandoned the Missouri River since last fall, and where they are at present, I am unable to say; I could not learn from either their friends or enemies; but it is presumed that they are some place in the Blackhills or on the Great Platte. During the last winter a war party belonging to the nation came on the Yellowstone below the Big Horn, where they fell in with three men belonging to the A. Fur Co. who they treacherously killed. Two of these men had been dispatched from Fort Cass in the morning with the express to go on to Fort Union. The third was a free man a veteran trapper, who was accompanying the others as far as a camp of White Hunters some short distance below the Fort. They scalped them and left part of the scalps of each tied to poles on the grounds of the murder. A large party of Crows went in pursuit of them the same evening or next day but could not overtake them. The names of the men killed are Rose, Menard, and Glass.

Jim Beckwourth, another legendary black explorer, mountain man, and friend of Rose saw the body of his friend and the two other men. He describes in his autobiography how he joined the group of Crow Indians pursuing the attackers:

> We rode up their bodies were scarcely cold... on we swept in pursuit of revenge. We traveled about thirty miles (each man leading his war-horse), and our saddle horses were beginning to tire, and we saw nothing of the enemy. Darkness would close over us, we feared, before we could overtake them. We then mounted our war-horses, which were as swift as the wind, and, leaving the saddle-horses behind, on we went faster than ever.

The attackers eluded Beckwourth and the Crows. Two other Aricara braves were later killed in retaliation for Menard, Glass and Rose.

Beckwourth, Du Sable, the Bonga brothers, and Rose were the kind of men made famous by the American author James Fenimore Cooper. In his *Leatherstocking Tales*, which included *The Last of the Mohicans*, *The Deerslayer*, and *The Pathfinder*, Cooper created a uniquely American hero. A leatherstocking was an early eighteenth century frontiersmen. Fearless. Resourceful. Wise to the land. His exploits seemed almost larger than life. His purpose was to make a way through the wilderness so that America could achieve its ''manifest destiny.''

Cooper's fictional heroes, Natty Bumppo and Hawkeye, were white as have been the traditional famous outdoorsmen — Davy Crockett, Daniel Boone, and Kit Carson. But courage, honesty, loyalty, and straightforwardness have no race. Americans can also take pride in the exploits of Beckwourth, Du Sable, Rose, and the Bonga brothers. There were other black trailblazers including John Brazeau, Isaiah Dorman, and York. Black scouts and interpreters were often sought by white fur companies and settlers because it was widely believed they had a "pacifying effect" on the Indians. Negotiations went smoother with blacks as mediators between Indians and whites.

By the end of the 1850's, the United States stretched from ocean to ocean, its geopolitical destiny substantially fulfilled. Government military forces had largely subordinated Native Americans in order to provide their lands for thousands of settlers from the east. Rising sectional tensions over the future of domestic slavery threatened to split the nation into two warring factions. Thousands of African Americans, descendants of Africans brought to the country by the original European colonizers, flocked to the territories and states where slavery was banned, seeking freedom and a choice to better themselves.

At the same time in Mexico, and the rest of Central and South America, the exploration and settlement phases had ended. Most of this area had won its freedom from Spain and abolished slavery.

The major exception was Brazil; larger than the continental United States, and with a bigger population of blacks, it won independence from Portugal in 1822. Brazil did not abolish slavery until 1888. European countries, however, maintained the bulk of their original island colonies.

Figure 35

Plantation scene — sugar

BLACKS AND THE OPENING OF THE AMERICAN WEST

Among the first explorers to land in what is now Oregon was a black sailor named Markus Lopeus. In August 1788, Captain Robert Gray commander of the sloop "Lady Washington" disembarked a foraging party on the headlands of Tillamook Bay. Lopeus and the other members of the small group had orders to locate fresh water to fill the ship's casks, game for the ship's galley, and wood to restore the ship's planking. The group was attacked by Indians, in the ensuing battle Lopeus lost his knife. As he attempted to recover his weapon he was killed by the Indians. To commemorate the demise of the young black sailor Gray named the landing spot Murderer's Harbor. Boston merchants had sent "The Lady Washington" to that area to collect a load of otter skins. Spanish and British competitors had already bought the best pelts. Gray finally collected enough skins, bartering a supply of American chisels for them with the Indians. He sailed to China, exchanged the skins for tea, and returned to Boston, becoming the first American sea captain to voyage around the world.

George Washington founded the town of Centralia, Washington (near U.S. 99 and the Chehalis River) in 1872. Washington was born in Virginia in 1817. In 1850, he and his foster parents (his mother had been a white woman who gave him up for adoption, his father was a black slave) traveled to the Oregon Territory. He married an attractive black woman, Mary Jane Coorness in 1867. His land lay in the path of the Northern Pacific Railroad and since he was an adroit farmer and businessman he decided to found a settlement halfway between Puget Sound and the Columbia River. To add impetus to the construction and habitation of his town, he sold lots at five dollars, donated money to build a cemetery, a church, and establish a fund to aid destitute settlers. During the Panic of 1893 Washington's magnanimity knew no bounds as he had wagon loads of supplies rushed in to feed the starving citizens. George Washington died in 1905.

Manuel Lopes, the first black resident of Seattle, Washington was a pioneer in other ways as well. He was Seattle's first barber. Lopes also imported the city's first barber's chair; it came by way of Cape Horn all the way around the tip of South America. Born in Africa, Lopes sailed from New Bedford, Massachusetts to Seattle. He also owned a restaurant and boarding house. He died in 1895.

In nearby Montana, Mary Fields, a black woman whose frame resembled a six foot block of carved ebony, wrote her own brand of history with a gun and a bull whip. Mary Fields, originally from Tennessee, came West, and worked as a nurse for the Ursuline nuns at Saint Peter's Convent in Cascade, Montana. She left the mission and opened a string of businesses including a restaurant and a stage and freight line. It was reported that the reason she left the mission was because of a dispute with the bishop — Mary and some anonymous gentleman had a disagreement and, in true western fashion, the inevitable shootout followed. The bishop said that it was poor form for a lady working in a mission to engage in shooting scrapes; Mary didn't think so and quit.

One night while hauling freight, wolves attacked her wagon. Her team of horses bolted, the wagon capsized and Mary plus the supplies were spilled on the hard Montana ground. All that night she maintained a lonely vigil; kept awake by the call of the wolves and in a display of magnificent shooting she kept the wolves at bay with the help of her trusty shotgun and pistol. In 1895, she accepted a job carrying the United States mail (she was

Figure 36

Settlers crossing the Red River in Texas, c. 1874

the second female stagecoach driver in the American West). She soon had to stop her excellent mail delivery service; the rigors of the trip were beginning to tell on Mary Fields. She was over sixty years old.

A decade later Mary was running a thriving laundry business in Cascade, Montana. In her spare time she frequented the local saloon where she smoked cigars and downed "old redeye" in full equality with the men. There was a singular incident before her death that personifies Mary's spirit.

Mary accosted a gentleman outside the saloon, who had repeatedly failed to pay his bill. Mary calmly approached the gentleman and then knocked him to the ground with one punch. Of the incident she later told her friends that the satisfaction of hitting the reprobate in the jaw had settled his bill. Tough and formidable, Mary was much like the frontier in which she lived. She died in 1914 and was buried in the Hillside Cemetery in Cascade, Montana.

Isaiah Dorman, a black scout and interpreter for the Army lost his life while part of the cavalry under the command of Major Marcus Reno at the Little Big Horn River in 1876. Reno was attached to the command of General Custer when he and his troops were massacred.

In Salt Lake City, Utah, at the entrance to Emigration Canyon, stands a monument commemorating the first Mormon settlers to arrive at the site of what is today the heart of the Mormon religion. Along with the name of Brigham Young and one hundred forty three white settlers are inscribed the names of three black pioneers who were in the first Mormon wagon caravan. Their names were Oscar Crosby, Hark Lay and Green Flake.

Many Mormon settlers, in their successive migratory waves toward Utah, carried blacks. A group of fifty-seven white Mississippi Mormons traveling to Utah in 1848 carried with them a total of thirty-five blacks.

Liz Flake, a black female slave, accompanied the family of her Mormon master from Nauvoo in Illinois to Salt Lake City in 1848 and eventually to San Bernadino, California in 1851. During these months on the trail her master and mistress died and Liz, instead of deserting the three white children that had been left behind, cared for and raised them, though only a teenager herself.

Liz Flake later married Charles H. Rowan, a successful black San Bernadino businessman and began to raise a family of her own.

Since the exploits of Estevanico, blacks had played an almost continual role in the history of Texas. A Spanish Census of 1792 listed 263 black males and 186 black females among the 1600 residents of Texas.

Moses Austin, who paved the way for the peaceful American settlement of Texas, began his journey to that country in 1820 accompanied only by his black slave, Richmond. After his father died, Stephen Austin carried on the work of colonization. By 1825, three hundred families of Austin's first contract, the original settlers, had formed a community of 1,800 of whom 443 were black slaves.

During the Texas struggle for independence from Mexico black men like Greenbury Logan also answered the call to arms.

Greenbury Logan wrote a poignant letter to the Texas state legislature describing how

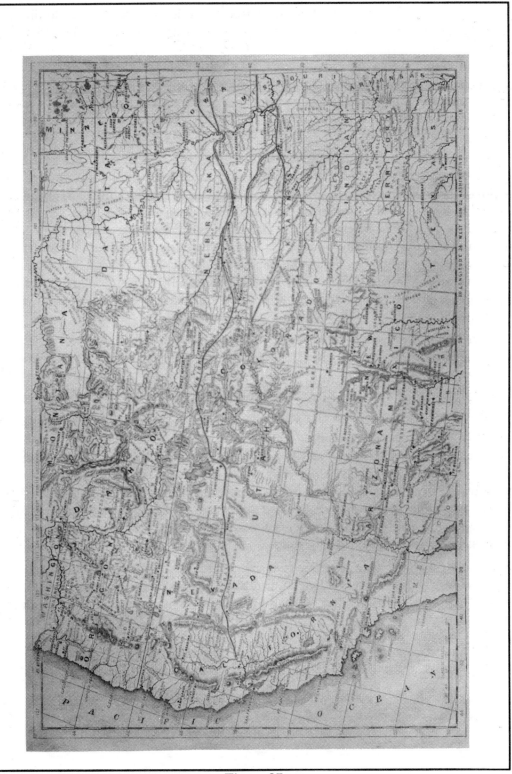

Figure 37

The Western frontier, c. 1867

due to wounds suffered in Texas' War for Independence he was too disabled to till his land and had been (as all other Texas blacks) denied his rights as a citizen. Even though Logan had been personally invited to settle in Texas by "Col. Austin" in 1831, the state legislature refused to grant him a tax exemption. A black man named Henrick Arnold was a scout for the American armies during the war between Texas and Mexico. Another, African American, Sam McCullough, was wounded at the battle of Goliad. A black slave of Col. W. B. Travis fought at and survived the Alamo, while Santa Ana, the besieging Spanish general, had a black valet.

Five years prior to his death at the Alamo, Jim Bowie and one of his slaves were in a party that fought off a Commanche attack near San Antonio. Bowie's slave, covered by the fire of the white men, darted to a stream and brought water back to the thirsty men. Jim Bowie had been a very successful slave trader. Between 1818 and 1820, he and his brother made $65,000 on blacks bought at Galveston Island for a dollar a pound, (a 150-pound man sometimes bringing as much as $1000 when they resold him in Louisiana). Had it not been for the timely information supplied by a black spy, General Sam Houston could have conceivably lost the battle of San Jacinto in April 1836. According to legend, he was also helped by a black woman in whose honor the song "Yellow Rose of Texas" was later written.

Aaron Ashworth moved to Texas in 1833, two decades later he had accumulated 2,570 head of longhorn cattle in east Texas. He owned the largest "spread" in both Orange and Jefferson counties (near Beaumont Texas).

Between 1846 and 1860 the number of black slaves in Texas rose from 38,753 to 180,682. Free black immigration was restricted.

In 1870, Afro-Americans comprised ten percent of the state legislature. Five years later nine black members of that same body helped to write the present constitution of the state of Texas. From Reconstruction until today, black Texas legislators have distinguished themselves. Early black legislators such as Texas state senators G.T. Ruby and Matt Gaines, along with Representatives Richard Allen and Alexander Asberry pushed bills that fought injustice, surveyed state resources, constructed a state pension law for veterans, built roads, and battled segregation.

The Lone Star State was also home to many of the 8,000 black cowboys that existed during the days of open range and long cattle drives. Bill Pickett, the inventor of the rodeo event called bulldogging and star of Zack Miller's 101 Wild West show, was born in Texas in 1870.

THE BLACK WESTERN EXODUS

Black Americans living in the South during the final phase of Reconstruction needed no crystal ball to tell then they were on the verge of losing their freedom. By this time the Democratic Party had regained Alabama, Arkansas and Mississippi. In the next year the Democratic Party backed by powerful former Confederate soldiers and sympathizers assumed command of Florida, South Carolina and Louisiana. As the dark veil of intolerance, bigotry and oppression spread over their social, economic and political lives, African Americans by the tens of thousands looked west as their only hope.

The fertile midwestern states of what is now Kansas, Nebraska and even Iowa had beckoned blacks before and during the Civil War. Pearl Street in Sioux City, Iowa, once the city's primary artery, is named for a black woman pioneer who more than a century ago arrived by boat and became a local legend for her skill with the skillet.

A black Civil War veteran, Henry Riding had a prosperous career as an Iowa farmer, He once forced the railroad off his land with his rifle and then made the firm pay him $21,000 for the use of the right of way. On another occasion, he shocked the residents of Sioux City, when he had his tombstone erected while he was in excellent health. "Aunty" Wooden was another black Iowa pioneer who gained fame with her skillet. Her popularity stemmed from a succulent dish of possum that only she could prepare. Both Clinton, Iowa and Sioux City were havens for fugitive slaves coming from Missouri.

The starting place for many westbound wagon trains, Missouri, included in its black population wagon maker Hiram Young whose prairie schooners each carried three quarters of a ton of goods down the Santa Fe and Oregon Trails.

It was, however, Kansas and Nebraska that beckoned to most of the discontented southern blacks. Two miles west of where the Rook and Graham County lines meet, blacks constructed the settlement of Nicodemus, Kansas, in 1877. The settlement, northwest of the town of Great Bend, was named after a black slave, who long ago, had predicted the Civil War. Kansas, in 1858 passed a "personal liberty" law and by 1860 there were over 189 free blacks in the state.

In 1879, the heretofore black trickle to the midwest became a flood. Led by black men like Benjamin "Pap" Singleton at least 40,000 blacks fled the South. But the land their grandfathers and grandmothers had been brought to in captivity, their descendants could not leave in peace. In May 1879, for example, James Chalmers and a group of his southern cronies blocked the Mississippi River by threatening to sink all vessels conveying blacks west. The owners of the endangered ships promptly stranded 1,500 blacks along the banks of the river. It required the threat of government force to make the transportation companies resume service. Time after time whites tried to turn the black migrants back. It was these attempts to stop black migration that formed the basis for the motion picture "Buck and the Preacher" in the early 1970s.

Once African Americans arrived in the midwest, a rude shock often awaited them. Many times they could not secure decent jobs and housing and they sometimes met with hostility from the Indians (to whom it seemed another attempt to crowd others in and them out) and whites (who viewed the large number of blacks as a job threat). A party of 150 blacks from Mississippi were forcibly ejected from Lincoln, Nebraska.

There were those among the white community who did extend a hand in friendship to the "Exodusters." They helped the blacks build homes and then provided them with jobs. The Governor of Kansas informed a 100-man delegation of black migrants that they could expect help from the state government.

In Nebraska, that state's 1866 constitution gave the vote to whites only. The next year when the state joined the Union blacks were granted suffrage but many were threatened with violence unless they stayed away from the voting booths in Omaha and Nebraska City. With the passage of two decades, blacks began to fully participate in the political and educational life in the state. Tom Cunningham was a black police officer in Lincoln. Dr. M.O. Ricketts was one of six blacks elected to the state legislature and the Shores family of Custer County, Nebraska was among the most affluent in the area.

African Americans in Kansas faced the same problems as their brothers and sisters in Nebraska. Early black settlers (c.1864) had to fight Irish immigrants, apathy, and vacillating attitudes from the white public. Black citizens also organized their own somewhat financially limited relief organization to aid other blacks. Eventually the barriers crumbled, black farmers established themselves and black cowboys rode to and raised hell in Kansas (just as their white counterparts did).

The first man thrown in the Abilene City jail was black and this same black trail cook was the first to break out of it. The first man killed in Dodge City was a black man named Tex. One of the slickest, most eloquent con-men in Dodge was black — Ben Hodges — and another black man, Henry Hilton owned a ranch only a few hours ride from the town.

By 1880, the black exodus to the midwest was in its final phases. The migrating blacks had found much of the land already taken and by this time there were already more blacks than could be employed. Undeterred, many African-Americans moved into Colorado and the other states surrounding the Indian territory of Oklahoma.

In the Central City Opera House in Central City, Colorado you can still see the chair commemorating "Aunt Clara" Brown. She is thought to have been the first black female resident of Colorado. "Aunt Clara" died in 1877 as she reached her eightieth birthday. A Virginia born slave, she watched her husband and children sold into slavery in Missouri. "Aunt Clara" gained her freedom through her master's will. She traveled through Missouri to Kansas and on to Colorado by wagon train. In Central City she opened the territory's first laundry and she organized the town's first Sunday school.

Spurred by her burning desire to reunite her family, she in 1866, used the ten thousand dollars she had saved, to search for and bring back to Colorado over thirty of her relatives. She remained in Central City performing charitable works and shortly before her death she was reunited with her daughter; the only member of her immediate family she ever saw again.

She was buried with honors by the Colorado Pioneers Association of which she was a proud and dedicated member. Her chair was dedicated in 1932 and a bronze plaque at the Saint James Episcopal Church relates how she freely let her home be used for worship before the church was built.

Another famous black Coloradan was Barney Ford, a businessman active during the days of the gold strike. Ford went to Colorado along with five other blacks to prospect for

Figure 38

Black and White gold miners in California

gold. Several miles southeast of the town of Breckinridge the six men began to prospect on a gentle rise of land the local whites simultaneously named "Nigger Hill" (Renamed Barney Ford Hill).

Once the blacks discovered gold they were driven off their diggings and because of the Dred Scott decision, i.e., blacks are not citizens, they have no rights which white men were bound to respect, they could not file a claim to legally protect their property.

Barney Ford was a former slave who had fled to Chicago, worked in the Illinois Underground Railroad, established a hotel in Nicaragua and successfully lobbied against Colorado's discriminatory suffrage laws. Ford and several other black Colorado pioneers, among them W.J. Hardin, Ed Sanderlin and H.O. Wagoner, started the state's first adult education program. Ford also owned several businesses in Denver. Ford owned and operated the spacious Inter-Ocean Hotel on Market Street between 15th Street and 16th Street, the People's Restaurant on Blake Street and a small barbershop.

Barney Ford was the first black man in Colorado to serve on a state jury. He died in Denver in 1902 and he and his wife are buried in the Riverside Cemetery.

Other black settlers in Colorado included Ferdinand Schavers, one of Abraham Lincoln's bodyguards, and Dr. Justina Ford who delivered thousands of children in the area around Denver and purchased a home there that has been converted into a black western museum.

In Colorado as elsewhere in the West blacks found themselves on both sides of the law. Willie Kenard was a U.S. Marshal in Yankee Hill, Colorado. H.O. Wagoner was the first black sheriff of Arapaho County, Colorado. Dan Diamond, a black desperado, broke out of the Denver County Jail (early 1870's) stole a horse and rode 24 miles before being captured, and the last man publicly hung in Denver was a black man, Andy Green.

In Idaho and Wyoming black pioneers and cowboys made a name for themselves. The Idaho Territory was first explored by Lewis and Clark, and York was probably the first black to visit the state. Southeast of that state in Cheyenne, Wyoming, Barney Ford opened another branch of his Inter-Ocean hotels and W.J. Hardin served in the state legislature. A black cowboy named Thornton Biggs who worked for Ora Haley's Two Bar Brand, established quite a reputation as a ladies' man among the girls at Susie Parker's house on Front Street in Laramie.

On April 22, 1889, a three million acre tract of former Indian land in what soon became Oklahoma was opened to homesteaders. The blast of the bugle at noon signaled the beginning of a flood tide of humanity into land previously held by Native Americans. Fifty thousand came the first day.

Between 1890 and 1910, twenty-five black communities were founded in Oklahoma. The reasons for black settlements in Oklahoma were basically the same that had spawned the "Black Exodus" ten years earlier. There was one striking difference, however: Blacks by this time had realized that the idea of the "melting pot" for them at least, was a dream deferred. Oklahoma was their hoped for Utopia, a place where they could establish all-black communities and live in peace with their white neighbors on terms of "separate but equal" equality.

The proudest black showpiece in Oklahoma was the all-black town of Boley. Boley had

Figure 39

William Alexander Leidesdorff

a population of four thousand and it was built on eighty acres of land. The town had the tallest building between Oklahoma City and Okmulgee and its proud paper, the *Boley Progress*, instilled in its citizens ideals of self-help and racial pride. Langston, Oklahoma was another all-black town in the state.

By the time Oklahoma was admitted to the Union in 1907 the hopes of its black citizens had been annihilated. The southern-influenced Democratic party gained political control of the legislature and the political aspirations of the blacks died. In 1907, the state adopted Jim Crow streetcar and railroad laws, three years later the state passed a discriminatory grandfather clause and in 1915 even the telephone booths were segregated. Against the weight of the oppressive laws, African American citizens could do little but grit their teeth and intensify their struggle for complete equality in a nation that was then on the verge of making the world safe for democracy during World War I.

Thousands of black men and women heard the cry of gold in California and they came to seek their fortune. One black gold miner was Waller Jackson who sailed around Cape Horn from Boston and mined at Downieville, California. Many other black Forty-Niners followed in his wake. Alvin Coffey crossed the continent in a wagon train in 1849 and soon earned five thousand dollars in the mines and seven hundred dollars working at nights. In spite of this he was sold and bought before he could purchase the freedom of his family. But by 1860, the Coffey family was free and were wealthy residents of Tehama County, California. Coffey was the only black member of the Society of California Pioneers.

Dozens of black Californians labored in the mining camps and dug in the earth at places like Downieville, Tuttlestown, Negro Bar (Folsom Lake), Spanish Flat and Auburn Ravine. Two Afro-Americans rode the California circuit of the Pony Express. George Monroe, himself the son of an early black gold miner, rode between Merced and Mariposa. William Robinson rode from Stockton to the nearby mines.

By 1850, the year California became a state, approximately 960 black Americans had come to California either as slaves or freeman. Twelve lived in Los Angeles. The Golden State was no racial utopia. The black men and women who grew prosperous and contributed to its history did so in a difficult and dangerous social and legal environment.

Between the time California was admitted as a state and the start of the American Civil War, the Fugitive Slave Law was vigorously enforced, blacks were denied the right to testify in court against white males, black migration to the state was forbidden (repealed a year later), and the state passed a stringent anti-fugitive slave bill.

Among the many black Americans to make an early contribution to the history of Los Angeles was Biddy Mason, a female ex-slave who took care of her master's livestock as they trekked across the country. When she arrived in Los Angeles, Biddy set herself up in a small business and began to buy parcels of land in what is now downtown "L.A." She also opened the city's first day nursery for orphans and poor children. Biddy Mason died in 1891.

Other blacks to achieve fame in "El Pueblo de Nuestra Senora la Reina de Los Angeles de Porciuncula" (the name given the settlement by the Spanish governor Felipe de Neve, it means the town of Our Lady the Queen of the Angels of the Porcuincula) were A.J. Jones who constructed the first "brick block" at First and San Pedro Streets and soon after became the city's premiere black capitalist and John Donnell, who owned a black-smith shop.

Of tremendous importance and accomplishment in San Francisco's early history was the black sailor and merchant William A. Leidesdorff. Born in St. Croix, Virgin Islands, Leidesdorff left the island for California after an unsuccessful "affair of the heart." A shrewd businessman, he piloted his 160-ton schooner "Julia Ann" into San Francisco's spacious bay in 1841. After trading between Hawaii and San Francisco for several years, Leidesdorff, sold his ship and built the city's first hotel (appropriately called the City Hotel) at the corner of Clay and Kearny Streets. Among Leidesdorff's many other hold-ings in the area were his Rio del Rancho Americano, a thirty-five thousand acre estate, a large warehouse near the waterfront and several acres of additional land. He inaugurated the city's first horse race and introduced its first steamship. In 1845, Leidesdorff was ap-pointed a U.S. subconsul to Mexican California. Leidesdorff was a member of the city council and headed the city's first school committee. After his death in 1848, Leidesdorff was interred beneath the floor of the Old Mission Dolores, where even today you may view his crypt plate placed among the tiles. At the foot of California Street, a short street has been named in his honor.

Two of the most famous Afro-Americans in San Francisco's history were Mammy Pleasant and George Washington Dennis. In ante-bellum San Francisco, Mary Ellen Pleasant, owner of a string of brothels which catered to some of the cream of the city's society raised over $40,000 for John Brown's raid on Harper's Ferry. Mammy Pleasant, a born civil rights activist, sued the city streetcar company for treating her rudely and traveled into the interior of the state rescuing slaves in open defiance of the Fugitive Slave Law of 1850. She acquired a large fortune and lost it before her death. Her grave is in the Tucolay Cemetery in Napa, California and her headstone is marked: "Mother of Civil Rights in California. Friend of John Brown."

George Washington Dennis was a black entrepreneur in true California style. A decade before the Civil War he owned some of the city's most valuable real estate, the blocks bound by Post, O'Farrell, Hyde and Larkin Streets, plus those bound by Post, Sutter, Scott and Divisadero. Dennis also owned the city's first coal yard. For his wife and ten children he built a residence on Bush Street.

Miffin W. Gibbs, a former San Francisco carpenter and businessman, rose through the ranks of California society to establish one of the state's first black newspapers, *Mirror of the Times*. He later became the first black judge in United States history.

After the Civil War, Allan Allensworth founded Allensworth, California, an all black town. Allensworth's home, its town school, and a museum still stand. The town is north of Bakersfield, California.

Twenty-three hundred miles west of California lie the Hawaiian islands. Blacks arrived there before the missionaries did in the 1820s. A seaman called Black Jack sailed there in the 1790s. Another black sailor, Antony Allen, stepped ashore in 1810 and stayed. He opened a tavern and the island's first bowling alley. A black woman, Betsy Stockton, ar-rived as a servant to a group of missionaries. She established one of Hawaii's first public schools.

In 1896, gold was discovered in Alaska and the possibility of quick wealth attracted numbers of blacks. One of them was Mattie Crosby who lived to be one of the oldest residents black or white of Fairbanks, Alaska. Large numbers of blacks again went to Alaska during World War II to build the Alcan Highway. Stretching 1,500 miles from British Columbia through the Yukon to Fairbanks, the Alcan Highway is one of the great unknown construction projects of World War II.

This is a list of major expeditions, towns, or topographical points in which black Americans participated or discovered in the American West:

Western topography is studded with undeniably black place names honoring black explorers or settlers, for example: Negro Creek Texas, Negro Canyon California (in honor of a black named Robert Owen), Negrohead Mountain, California, Negro Head Arizona, Nigger Mesa, New Mexico, (because of a shoot out involving a black man); Nigger Canyon California (Orange County), Coon Hollow, Wyoming (because a black named Turner lived in the vicinity); Coon Hollow, Washington (now part of Seattle). Texas has at least thirty three such locations including Negro Liberty Settlement, Negro Bend, Negro Gully, and Negro Crossing.

1800 — Philip Nolan Expedition:

As early as 1797, Nolan, a white Kentuckian, had come to Texas for the purpose of gathering wild horses. Basically a trader, Nolan made several trips into the region taking along what appeared to the Spanish government to be instruments for mapping the countryside. On the basis of these suspicions, charges were filed, Nolan was accused of being a spy and his arrest was ordered (1799) if he should ever return to Texas.

In October of the next year Nolan and twenty men, including a black man named Caesar left Natchez, Mississippi for Texas. They fought a Spanish patrol in Louisiana (three men King, Adams, and Richards deserted) and traded among the Indians of East Texas for horses to continue their travels. With Ceasar acting as a cook and intermediary with the Indians the group explored as far into the interior as the Red River.

On March 21, 1801, upon returning to their camp, which was probably somewhere between the present cities of Waco and Mexia, they were attacked by a company of Spanish soldiers sent from Nacogdoches (blacks were in that towns original settlement party) to find them. Philip Nolan was killed, three were seriously wounded and three successfully escaped. Ten of the Americans including Caesar were captured and eventually taken to Mexico City.

Six years later, the Spanish king handed down an edict that said one of each five of the captives must be hanged. At this time there were only nine left and the administrators in Mexico City ruled that the death of one would satisfy the decree. Each of the men threw dice on a drumhead to determine their fate. Fate frowned upon Ephraim Blackburn. He was executed in the province of Chihuahua on November 11, 1807. Caesar and the rest of the survivors were then sentenced to an additional ten years in prison. That is the last we hear of the fate of Caesar or the others.

1804 — Lewis and Clark Expedition:

President Thomas Jefferson had long been interested in the lands west of the Mississippi River. In 1803, after receiving a $2,500 appropriation from Congress, he chose his former secretary Meriwether Lewis to head an exploration party into the lands of the newly bought Louisiana Purchase.

Lewis picked as his co-commander Captain William Clark who had once commanded an army unit in which Lewis had served. Both went about organizing a semi-military exploring force that included fourteen soldiers, two Frenchmen, nine Kentucky backwoodsmen, and a black slave named York. Their mission was to gain a knowledge of Western topography and natural resources and to search for the Indian tribes that inhabited the region.

Later, an Indian woman Sacajawea and her interpreter husband were added to the group. Laden with provisions, weapons and trinkets for trading, the intrepid band embarked on a journey that was to last two years, four months and nine days. York, the only black on the expedition, is referred to throughout Clark's journal as a "servant" but this is merely a polite euphemism — York was in fact Clark's slave. York's purpose on the trip was to act as an overall handyman and cook. Ultimately he began to act as a kind of buffer or intermediary between the curious and potentially hostile Indians and the white members of the Lewis and Clark expedition.

York first appears in Clark's journal on Tuesday, June 5, 1804: "which we named Sand C., here my servant York Swam to the sand bar to geather Greens for our Dinner, and returned with a sufficient quantity wild creases (cresses) or Tung grass [sic]."

As they moved through the hostile environment tempers flared and initial enthusiasm lagged. A short time later this entry appeared in the journal: "...about the only members of the party who could be counted on to do as told were Clark's servant York and Lewis' big dog, Scannon." It was not until the Indians began to show a more than passing interest in York that Lewis and Clark realized what potential for good relations they had in the person of this over six foot, two hundred pound black man. York too, realized his importance and played it for all it was worth as illustrated in this extract from the journal: "... Of the other members of the exploring party, York, Captain Clark's Negro servant, attracted the most attention from both the Hidatsa and Mandan Indians. They had never before seen a Negro and did not know quite what to make of him. York himself, a dark corpulent man, tried to make the Indians believe he had been wild like a bear and tamed. One Eye, the principal Hidatsa Chief, examined York closely, spit on his hand and rubbed the Negro's skin, believing that he might be a painted white man. Possibly this Indian's reaction to York survives in the name for Negro in the languages of some of the upper Missouri tribes, which may be translated as black white man."

Another similar entry stated: "But they (Lewis and Clark) must wait while the air gun was shot or one of the men went into a jig or someone struck up a tune on the violin to keep the Indians in a negotiating mood. When they ran out of diversions, a display of York's black skin and wiry curls made a good show. "We have learnt by experience" Lewis explained, "that to keep the savages in good humor their attention should not be

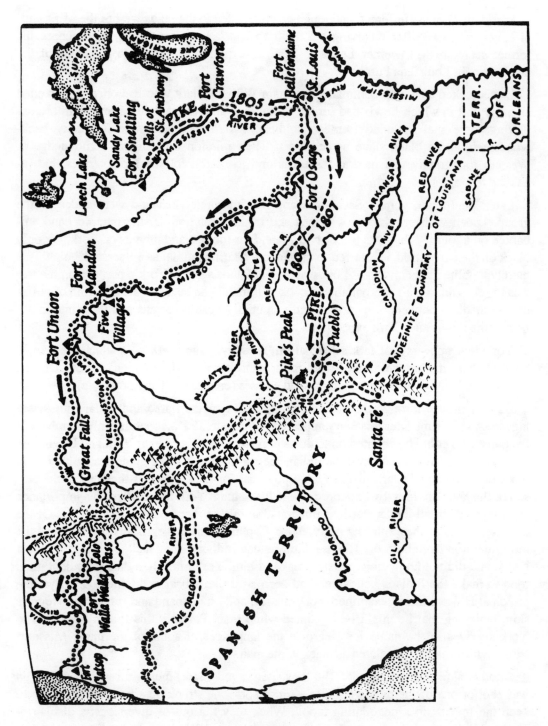

Figure 40

Map of the Lewis and Clark expedition. Pike's expedition had no black members but was the first government expedition in the area later explored by the Bonga family.

worried by too much business... matters should be enlivened with what is new and enter-
taining.''

York's role in the expedition grew and so did his popularity among the various Indian
nations: ''River Maropa 9th of October 1804. Tuesday ... Sorry (several) Canoes of Skins
passed down from the 2 villages a short distance above, and many came to view us all
day, much astonished at my black servant, who did not lose the opportunity of (display-
ing) his powers and Strength... this nation never saw a black man before.'' ''...15th of October Monday 1804...Those people (recares) are much pleased with my black
servant.''..''Sunday 28th of October 1804... we made up the presents and entertained
several curious Chiefs whome, wished to see the boat which was verry curious to them
viewing it as great medison, as they also viewed my black servant. [sic]''

The expedition spent the winter in the villages of the Mandan Indians over 1500 miles
from the start of their journey. These villages were located near the present site of Bismarck, North Dakota.

The next spring they reached the forks of the Missouri and they named the three rivers
the Jefferson, the Madison and the Gallatin. Each time Lewis and Clark encountered a
band of Indians with whom they sought to negotiate, York was called upon to repeat his
performance: ''Friday, August 15, 1805...I (Lewis) had mentioned to the chief several
times that we had with us a woman of his nation who had been taken prisoner by the Min-
netaries, and that by means of her I hope to explain more fully than I could do signs, some
of the party had also told the Indians that we had a man with us who was black and had
short curly hair. This excited their curiosity very much, and they seemed quite as anxious
to see this monster as they were the merchandise which we had to barter for their horses.''

The Indians were amazed at York's size and strength and he (York) realized as did
Lewis and Clark that his actions were facilitating their trek through these uncharted lands.
As a kind of ambassador, York's first duty was to break the barriers of suspicion and hostility western Indians often held towards these strange interlopers. Another entry in the
journal reads: ''... The Indians came and were amazed by Clark's giant servant, York. He
was the first black man they had ever seen. The natives ''all flocked around and examined
him from top to toe,'' Clark wrote York enjoyed the situation immensely. ''He carried on
the joke himself and made himself more terrible then we wished him to doe. [sic]'' He
told the Indians he was a wild animal Clark had captured and tamed. A horde of little boys
followed him at a safe distance wherever he went. York loved it. He would turn and bare
his teeth or growl and the small fry would scatter screaming, only to gather again immediately when he turned his back.

Another interesting facet of York's unique importance to the expedition is contained in
this entry: ''...The two captains advanced and shook hands with the chief, who commanded his people to refrain from any evil doing toward them. The white men removed
their pack saddles from their horses and sat down on the ground. The chief said: ''They
had no robes to sit on. Some Indians have stolen them. Bring them robes.'' Buffalo skins
were brought but instead of sitting on them, the white man threw them about their
shoulders. One of them had a black face, and the Indians said among themselves. ''See his
face is painted black.'' They are going to have a scalp dance. The Indians (the expedition
was then among the flathead Indians) thought York was a white man who had painted

himself black with charcoal. In those days it was the custom for Flathead warriors, when returning home from battle, to prepare themselves before reaching camp. Those who had been brave and fearless, the victorious ones in battle, painted themselves in charcoal. So the black man, they thought, had been the bravest of his party.

After nearly three years in the wild hinterlands of America, the Lewis and Clark expedition, ably assisted by York and the Indian guide, Sacajawea, reached their destination, the Pacific Coast. By the time they left the mouth of the Columbia River they had erected Ft. Clatsop, peacefully met with the Ottawas at a place they named Council Bluffs, established friendly relations with the Mandans, Arikaras, Dakotahs, Nez Perces, Shoshones, and Flatheads, and added an incredible chapter of daring and resourcefulness to the saga of early American exploration. The expedition returned overland, the party splitting so that Lewis went down the Marias River, and Clark went down the Yellowstone. They rejoined at the mouth of the Yellowstone and entered St. Louis, Missouri on September 23, 1806. They had become the first American expedition to cross the continent to the Pacific Coast. It had been a journey of 7,689 miles.

York's prowess and athletic ability had manifested itself more than once during their travels. He had swum, danced in front of the Indians, suffered from the pounding of the elements as a full member of the expedition, been almost killed by a maddened bull buffalo and on one occasion saved the life of William Clark, Sacajawea and her baby. The expedition was of immeasurable value in opening the entire area to settlement and development.

Of York's fate, history is not certain. It is known that he returned with Clark to Louisville, where he was hired out to a local family so that he could be near his wife. Eventually, William Clark did free him and buy him a wagon and six horses. With this material according to Clark, York established a freight line between Richmond and Nashville. York, according to this same account, proved to be such a bad businessman that he begged the southern born Clark to take away his freedom and again make him a slave. Clark ended this version of York's demise by saying that as York was traveling to rejoin him in St. Louis. He died of cholera prior to reaching his destination.

Clark's story is countered by the narrative rendered by a white trapper, Zenas Leonard. In 1832, while trading among the Crow Indians, Leonard had encountered a black chief who was a skillful warrior and exercised a fluent command of the Crow language. The black chief told Leonard that he had accompanied the Lewis and Clark expedition, returned home with Clark and ultimately returned to the West and settled among the Crow.

There are other stories, some say that York had a freight line out west, some say he remained in the South and became a successful businessman.

There can be no epitaph or closing anecdote to York's exploits. In a country where the names of Lewis and Clark are admired and have not been forgotten, where there are more statues to Sacajawea than almost any other woman of color, nothing could save York from virtual oblivion.

1820s — JEDEDIAH SMITH EXPEDITIONS

Jedediah Strong Smith was the first white explorer to cross the Great Salt Lake Desert and the Sierra Nevada Mountains. He was a respected mountain man, trader, and trapper who travelled with several blacks on his various journeys throughout the west. In August 1826, he led a 17-man party of trappers on a zigzag course southward from Bear Lake near the borders of what is now Utah and Idaho, to the Colorado River. One of the men on this journey was John Peter Ranne, a ''colored man.''

There was no hint of fall approaching in the arid land they crossed. The sun blazed unceasingly. The countryside was rocky and dusty. The ascent and descent of each hill and mountain tested man and beast. During this trip, Ranne became the first recorded black man to visit the state of Nevada. Shortly after the group reached the Colorado River, they camped with a group of friendly Mojave Indians and took stock of their situation. Over half of their horses were gone. But Smith and his men decided to go on. They were looking for a fabled river called the Buenaventura. According to the legends, its banks were thick with beavers and it flowed west through the mountains to the great ocean. Whoever found it would have control of rich trapping lands and a waterway to take furs east and bring supplies back to the west.

Smith, Ranne and the others pushed back into the searing Mojave Desert, crossed the rugged San Bernadino mountains, and hungry and weary, they limped into Southern California. Smith and his men were the first Americans to arrive in California by a land route from the east, the first to cross the Great Salt Lake Desert and the Sierra Nevada.

Surprised Mexican border officials immediately realized what the presence of these men meant. Whether they were settlers or trappers it would not be long before other Americans followed them. The United States government would then make demands for this rich territory in which so many of their citizens lived. Mexico was especially sensitive to any threat to its territory. Only five years earlier, Mexico itself had won its independence from Spain after 20 years of fighting.

Governor Jose Echeandia believed Smith and his party were spies at first. He later changed his mind after Smith and others convinced him that they had become lost and strayed into Mexican territory by accident. Echeandia released them and ordered them to go back the way they had come.

As soon as they were safely away from the Mexicans, Smith and his men, still looking for the Buenaventura, headed north through central California. When they reached the American river east of Sacramento, they went upstream hoping to cross the Sierras. It was May 1827. Snow still choked every path. There seemed to be no way through the mountains.

Smith divided his party taking two men for another try at the mountains. Ranne and the others remained behind at a camp back on the Stanislaus River. This time Smith successfully crossed the Sierras. It was a different journey. Smith and his men ate their horses after they ran out of food. When they ran out of water, they covered themselves with desert sand to save their sweat.

After travelling back to Bear Lake and collecting 18 new men, Smith started back to California. In Smith's new group was another black mountain man, Polette (or Polite)

Labross. This time, however, the Mojave Indians were not friendly. Seeking revenge after a battle with another party of trappers, the Indians attacked Smith and his men at the Colorado River. Labross and nine other men were killed. In September 1827, Smith and the eight survivors met the group he had left behind in California.

Helped by English and American ship captains in San Francisco, Smith got supplies for his men. In late December, they swung north. They trapped through the northern California mountains known as the Coast Range.

Along the tree-fringed banks of streams, each man carefully baited and set their underwater traps, smearing each with the sex-scent of a beaver. Early the next morning, each man checked his line of traps skinning each caught beaver. A pack of 60 pelts was worth a small fortune.

Somewhere along the Umpqua River, not long after the group had crossed into southern Oregon, they came to a level grassy plain where they set up camp. Indians attacked them. Ranne and twenty other men were killed. Only Smith and three other men survived. A few years later, Smith got out of the fur business and became a trader along the Santa Fe Trail. He was ambushed and killed near there by Comanches in 1831. He never found the Buenaventura.

Black trailblazers like Ranne and Labross shared the hardships of their white comrades and ultimately gave their lives in this nation's great westward movement. They were in the forefront of the American explorers who ventured to the far west. The trappings of civilization came much later. It was not until 1841 that the first emigrant wagon train left for California. The following year, the first settlers journeyed to a region of western North America between the Pacific Coast and the Rocky Mountains, then called the Oregon Country.

1842 — JOHN C. FREMONT EXPEDITIONS

Several blacks accompanied United States topographical surveyor John Charles Fremont "the Pathfinder" on at least three of his western explorations. During Fremont's first trip west he surveyed an overland wagon trail across the Rocky Mountains just before the era of the great wagon trains. The Oregon Trail was over 2,000 miles long beginning at the Missouri River, merging with the Santa Fe Trail and then branching off and rising slowly through six states before ending in what is now Washington State.

In his second journey in 1843-1844, Fremont mentioned "Jacob Dodson, a free young colored man of Washington City, who volunteered to accompany the expedition, and performed his duty manfully throughout the voyage." Dodson was eighteen years old in 1843 and is believed to have been a servant of Fremont's father-in-law, Senator Thomas Hart Benton of Missouri. Katz quotes Fremont and other members of the expedition as describing Dodson as "...strong and active and nearly six feet in height... expert as a Mexican with a lasso, superior to a mountaineer with the rifle, equal to either on horse or foot, and always a lad of courage and fidelity."

Katz also mentions the long, dangerous ride Fremont, Dodson and others made from Los Angeles to Monterey and back in nine days total. A distance of over seven hundred miles. I cite Katz, again: "another time...Fremont, Dodson and another man galloped 120

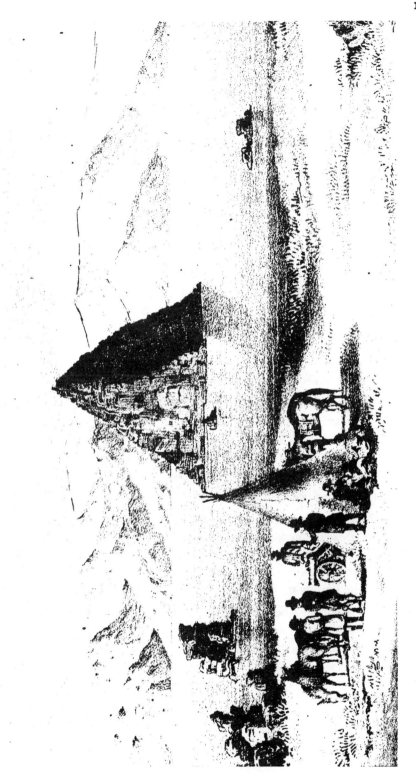

Figure 41
The Pyramid Lake (An illustration from Fremont's book)

miles in one day. Dodson was responsible for roping fresh horses when their steeds became exhausted.''

Fremont's second expedition left Missouri in May 1843 and travelled to Oregon. Dodson was among a party of trusted men Fremont chose for a trip along the Columbia River to Vancouver, across the border in Canada. After returning to Oregon, Fremont's party crossed into Nevada. Near where the Smoke Creek Desert meets the Virginia Mountains, they halted in front of a huge glistening body of water. Fremont named it Pyramid Lake; one hundred sixty-eight square miles in area, it is one of the largest lakes in the United States. Fremont, Dodson and the others were the first outsiders to see it.

By March of 1844, Fremont's expedition had survived a rugged winter, crossed the Sierras, and rested their horses at Sutter's Fort near Sacramento. During a snowstorm in the mountains, Dodson saved the life of a member of the expedition. Fremont and his men headed east through Nevada and Utah finally arriving in St. Louis Missouri. Fremont's trek kindled the interest of thousands of Americans to go west.

It is unclear precisely who accompanied Fremont in his third mission west in May 1845. There is no roster of participants. Dodson is believed to have ridden with him as well as several others. Fremont's third expedition found itself involved in the Bear Flag Revolt in California, a rebellion of American settlers against Mexican rule. The revolt began in Sonoma, California on June 14, 1846. Fremont and his men arrived eleven days later offering support to the rebels. The following year Dodson and Fremont made their famous ride from Los Angeles to Monterey and back.

Clashes between the United States and Mexico over American encroachment culminated in 1846 in the Mexican War. After two years of fighting, Mexico agreed to relinquish Arizona, New Mexico, Texas, Nevada, Utah, part of Colorado, and all of California to the United States in return for only fifteen million dollars.

Fremont led expeditions across the Rockies in 1848-1849 and 1853-1854.

Several historians mention other blacks who travelled with Fremont or served with him in California. Beasley mentions James Duff, a ''bodyguard or servant'' named Ben, Joe McAfee, Charles G. Gains, and Billy Gaston. Kenneth Goode lists Saunders Jackson. Rusco lists Tamas Towns and an unnamed black man mentioned in ''the accounts of at least three white immigrant parties going to southern California by way of Utah in 1849.''

Dodson crossed the Rocky Mountains a total of three times. In his later years, he returned to Washington, D.C. where he worked in the Senate Chambers. Less than two weeks after the Rebel bombardment of Fort Sumter, Dodson wrote to the Secretary of War offering to raise a force of three hundred blacks to defend the Nation's Capital. He was brusquely refused.

On April 13-15, 1986, CBS Television Network broadcast a seven-hour miniseries on the explorations of John Charles Fremont. The miniseries starred Richard Chamberlain as Fremont and was called ''Dream West.'' No blacks, however, were shown exploring or fighting alongside Fremont.

1844 — SIMMONS-BUSH PARTY REACH WASHINGTON STATE

One of the earliest American pioneers in the state of Washington, was a free black man named George W. Bush. J.A. Rogers described him as "the founder of the State of Washington." Bush had lived in Pennsylvania and later became a prosperous Missouri farmer and cattle trader. He and a white friend, Colonel M.T. Simmons decided to move to the Oregon country (stretching from California to Alaska) after Missouri had ordered all free blacks to leave the state. Bush, as the wagon train's guide and part financial backer, was a close friend to all the white settlers in the convoy. On the trail they made a vow not to settle anywhere Bush would be discriminated against because of his color.

They spent the winter along the Columbia River. Bush, his white wife and their five children along with Simmons and the rest of the party, decided to forsake Oregon and go north of the Columbia River and into British territory where he might receive fairer treatment from the local government and slavery was not permitted. The settlers halted their wagons on a grassy expanse and founded the city of Tumwater, Washington near Puget Sound. During his travels Bush had lost none of his business acumen, he established a land claim and became a skillful farmer. Bush built a home and established a farm on land known today as Bush Prairie. He was the only man in the Puget Sound area with a surplus of wheat during the bitter famine of 1852.

As the state's population grew, Bush continually proved himself to be a friend to the neighboring settlers. He lent money, tools, and advice. He opened his home to people travelling between the Columbia River and Puget Sound.

Two years after the Simmons-Bush party settled in the region, a treaty between the United States and Great Britain established the new territory of Washington's boundary on the 49th parallel (1846). To a large degree, the successful prosecution of the United States' claim was due to the presence of the Simmons-Bush party in that territory. The fact that a well-established community of Americans already existed in the area helped to defeat the British position. The territory of Washington was officially established in 1853. Washington achieved statehood in 1889. George Bush died in 1863. One of his sons raised a prized wheat crop (wheat is still one of the state's leading agricultural products) which was eventually exhibited at the Smithsonian Institution in Washington, D.C. Another son, William Owen Bush was elected to the Washington State House in 1889.

1850 — JAMES BECKWOURTH DISCOVERS BECKWOURTH PASS

James P. Beckwourth, born in Virginia around 1789, of a slave mother and a white Revolutionary War officer, grew to become a figure of prime importance in western exploration. Before Beckwourth discovered the California pass that bears his name, the then fifty-two year old black mountain man had already lived through a series of adventures rivaling anything conjured up by a Hollywood screen writer.

Beckwourth had come to St. Louis, Missouri, from Virginia, been a blacksmith's apprentice, grown restless, gone to New Orleans, and signed up as a scout for General Henry Ashley's Rocky Mountain expedition. One of the motivating factors accounting for Beckwourth's restlessness was a disaffection for slavery and his inability to effectively cope with a white supremacist society.

Figure 42
The author at Beckwourth Pass, California

Figure 43
James Beckwourth, explorer

While a member of Ashley's expedition, Beckwourth learned the rudiments of staying alive and making a living in the American wilderness. He soon mastered the arts of trapping, hunting, shooting, Indian fighting, shoeing horses and one of the most valuable traits of a true mountain man the ability to wildly exaggerate. In 1824, he was adopted by the Crow Indians, when an old squaw insisted he was her long lost son. To the Crow Indians the measure of a man was what he could do, not the color of his skin and Beckwourth did many things well.

In battle Beckwourth was utterly fearless and his fame as a crack shot spread throughout the neighboring tribes. He rose quickly to tribal leadership. The Crows called Beckwourth ''Morning Star,'' ''Medicine Calf,'' and later in honor of his exploits in battle, ''Bloody Arm'' (red with the blood of his enemies). The wanderlust again struck him in a few years and neither his Indian wives or the intrinsic quality of their lifestyle could stay his urge to move on. He served as an Army scout during the Third Seminole War in Florida. About 1842 Beckwourth founded the Gantt-Blackwell Fort at Pueblo, Colorado. In 1843 Beckwourth, accompanied by his Spanish wife, encountered John C. Fremont on one of his expeditions sixty miles east of the Rocky Mountains. During California's Bear Flag Rebellion he met General Kearny, who already well acquainted with the black man's exploits, asked for his assistance.

In April 1850 ''Jim'' Beckwourth discovered a passage through the Sierra Nevada mountain chain — the lowest passage through that mountain system north of the desert. This is how he described the pass in his autobiography:

> ''We proceeded in an easterly direction, and all busied themselves searching for gold; but my errand was of a different character: I had come to discover what I suspected to be a pass.
>
> It was the latter end of April when we entered upon an extensive valley at the northwest extremity of the Sierra Range. The valley was already robed in freshest verdure, contrasting most delightfully with the hugh snow clad masses of rock we had just left. Flowers of every variety and hue spread their variegated charms before us; magpies were chattering, and gorgeously-plumaged birds were caroling in the delights of unmolested solitude. Swarms of wild geese and ducks were swimming on the surface of the cool crystal stream, which was the central fork of the Rio de las Plumas, or sailed the air in clouds over our heads. Deer and antelope filled the plains, and their boldness was conclusive that the hunter's rifle was to them unknown. Nowhere visible were any traces of the white man's approach, and it is probable that our steps were the first that ever marked the spot... This, I at once saw, would afford the best wagon-road into the American Valley...''

Later, over the wagon road through the pass streamed thousands of settlers. Beckwourth personally guided many wagon trains through the pass. In one train was eleven-year-old Ina Coolbrith (later California's first poet laureate). She described Beckwourth as:

> A dark-skinned man dressed in a leather coat and moccasins, who wore his hair in two long braids twisted with colored cloth, riding without a

saddle. He rode the two Coolbrith girls through the pass on his horse. At the foot of the pass [she recalled] Beckwourth pointed forward and said, "Here is California, little girls, here is your kingdom."

"Beckwourth Pass," located between the Feather and Truckee rivers in California, was not only discovered by a black man; he returned to an adjacent meadow (Beckwourth Meadow) and established a combination hotel-trading post, the only such building then between that point and Salt Lake City:

In the Spring of 1852, I established myself in Beckwourth Valley...My house is considered the emigrant's landing place, as it is the first ranch he arrives at in the Golden State.

After opening his store near the pass he discovered, Beckwourth decided that the role of store-keeper was too sedentary. He bought himself a ranch in the nearby Feather River Valley, married again (for the fourth or fifth time) and moved to Denver, Colorado. While in Denver, Beckwourth got involved in an argument with another man, the argument wasn't concluded until the other man lay dead at Beckwourth's feet. The black mountain man was eventually acquitted on a plea of self-defense. He then decided to return to his friends and family among the Crow Indians. He married Sue, a young Indian woman.

According to one legend, the Crows invited Beckwourth to a tribal feast in an effort to convince him to again become their Chief. When he rejected their overtures, the Indians poisoned him. The Crows reasoned that if they could not have him as a live chief, they would at least keep his spirit.

Beckwourth, however, actually died of food poisoning at a lonely spot along the trail, two days journey from the nearest Crow village.

Colonel Henry Inman in his book, *The Old Sante Fe Trail*, summed up Beckwourth in the following portrait:

... It is an unquestioned fact that Beckwourth was the most honest trader among the Indians of all who were then engaged in the business. Kit Carson and Colonel Boone were the only Indian agents whom I ever knew or heard of that dealt honestly with the various tribes, as they were always ready to acknowledge, and the withdrawal of the former by the government was the cause of a great war, so also Beckwourth was an honest Indian trader.

He was a born leader of men, and was known from the Yellowstone to the Rio Grande, from Santa Fe to Independence, and in St. Louis...

In person, Beckwourth was of medium height and great muscular power, quick of apprehension, and with courage of the highest order. Probably no man ever met with more personal adventures involving danger to life, even among the mountaineers and trappers who early in the century faced the perils of the remote frontier. From his neck he always wore suspended a perforated bullet, with a large oblong bead on each side of it, tied in place with a single thread of sinew. This amulet he obtained while chief of the Crows, and it was his "medicine," with which he excited the superstition of his warriors.

His success as a trader among the various tribes of Indians has never been surpassed; for his close intimacy with them made him know what would best please their taste, and they bought of him when other traders stood idly at their stockades, waiting almost hopelessly for customers.

Beckwourth died in October 1866. The Crows, among whom he lived so long, buried him near their camp.

August 1, 1903, saw the end of the first transcontinental auto trip, the country linked by railroad was now linked, though rather tentatively, by rubber. The continental frontier was closed.

In 1909, a black, far in advance of the main body of explorers planted the flag on yet another frontier. A modern day Estevanico, Matthew Alexander Henson, was the first outsider to reach the North Pole.

CHAPTER 4

TO EVERY CORNER OF THE EARTH

During prehistoric times, in an unceasing search for land or fresh game, waves of black immigrants left Africa and settled in regions far from their native land. They established or helped to establish many far flung and nearly forgotten civilizations and empires. Some historians claim that because blacks were the first humans they were also the first explorers, placing the original stamp of humanity upon the vastness of the globe. Whatever the case, archeological evidence, ancient legends, and first-hand reports place African peoples in every corner of the earth.

In June, 1901, a French scientist found three levels of human remains in the Grimaldi caves in France. In the soil of the first two levels were the remains of a people known as Cro-Magnon. These remains were of a type first discovered in the Cro-Magnon cave near Les Eyzies, France. Cro-Magnon remains are close in appearance to those of modern Europeans. When French anthropologist Rene Verneau examined the skeletons at the bottom level and therefore the earliest of all three levels, he found that the remains were not those of modern Europeans. Marcellin Boule and Henry Vallois in their book, *Fossil Men*, report their findings on the "Grimaldi" skeletons:

> "When we compare the dimensions of the bones of their limbs, we see that the leg was very long in proportion to the whole arm; and that the lower limbs were exceedingly long relative to the upper limbs. Now these proportions reproduce, but in greatly exaggerated degree, the characteristics presented by the modern Negro. Here we have one of the chief reasons for regarding these fossils as Negroid, if not actually Negro."

Boule and Valois described the Grimaldi remains as having other skeletal characteristics of blacks: longer and higher skulls, broad faces, and large eye sockets. The discovery of the Grimaldi skeletons was then the latest in a series of finds showing black peoples to have inhabited Europe before modern Caucasians. Negroid or Africoid skeletons had been found from Portugal to Switzerland to eastern Europe. Anatomically these skeletons appear to be the first homo sapiens to have lived in Europe. They practiced burial rituals, cave painting, and sculpture. Their depictions of the female form show their women to have been built like modern San or Khoi Khoin women of South Africa. The hairstyles usually show a "peppercorn" arrangement where the hair grows in tight small curls. The figurines are incredibly lush and full-figured with large swinging breasts and protuberant stomachs and buttocks.

The Grimaldis arrived in Europe during the Aurignacian Age or Upper Stone Age about 40,000 B.C. Scientists generally believe that the Grimaldis appeared in Europe after Neanderthal Man and before Cro-Magnon who is believed to be the prehistoric ancestor of the modern European.

New finds are pushing the timetable of African arrival in Europe farther back in time. *The European*, a weekly newspaper published in England, reported a 1.6 million-year-old fossil find in Spain in its August 9, 1991 issue. Under the caption "Is This the First European?" the newspaper disclosed that:

> The unearthing of fragments of bone and primitive stone tools made by our earliest ancestors threaten to overturn long held theories that first migrations were from Africa via Asia some 700,000 years ago. The finds made by one of Spain's leading paleontologists suggest that early man

first made the journey across the Strait of Gibraltar from mankind's African birthplace at least a million years before.

The evidence for their existence has been excavated by Professor Joseph Gilbert, from a cave and from what was once the edge of a watering hole on the savannah that covered large areas of southern Spain. The bones, which include part of a cranium similar to fossils discovered in the world-famous Olduvai Gorge in Kenya, are among the oldest remains of early man ever found. The first European was not homo sapiens — modern man — but more closely related to homo habilis or homo erectus, his African contemporaries.

The article notes that during prehistoric times southern Spain was a kind of Africa extended comprised of "a huge semi-arid plain similar to African savannah ... as well as human bones, the dig has uncovered those of elephants, rhinos, dolphins, seals..."

Hundreds of miles to the northwest, in Ireland, legends describe its aboriginal race as short dark people called the Firbolgs. One of the semi-mythical pre-Celtic inhabitants of Ireland, the Firbolgs, meaning "skin boats" or "people of the bag" are credited with constructing large stone shelters throughout the country.

E. Cobhan Brewer and Ivor H. Evans, in *Brewer's Dictionary of Phrase and Fable*, believe that the Firbolgs were supplanted by the Milesians, the name given to the ancient Irish after a past king:

"...the true sons of Milesius, a fabulous king of Spain, conquered the country and repeopled it after exterminating the Firbolgs (the Aborigines)."

Another legend reports the Firbolgs were defeated by the Formarians and fled to Greece where they were captured and made slaves. In later times, according to the *History of the Kings of Britain*, by Geoffrey of Monmouth, Gormund, an African ruled parts of Ireland during the sixth century A.D.

Farther north of Ireland in Scandinavia, there are stories of early black people called Skraelings. In *African Presence in Early Europe*, edited by Ivan van Sertima, author Legrand H. Clegg describes research from various sources indicating that a group of small black peoples lived in Scandinavia and Greenland around 1300 A.D. Contemporary authors and observers called them "Skraelings," a Norse word for small.

J.A. Rogers, in *Sex and Race* and *Nature Knows No Color Line*, Professor Edward Scobie in *Black Britannia*, David MacRitchie in *Ancient and Modern Britons*, and Gerald Massey in *A Book of the Beginnings* are among the authors to provide evidence of a prehistoric African presence in Great Britain.

The Roman historian Tacitus writing about 100 A.D. in *Agricola* and *Annals* tells the story of the Silures or Black Celts of Britain with their unusually curly hair, short stature, and dark skins. The Silures occupied southern Wales and fiercely resisted Roman domination. The Silures are believed to have arrived in Wales in Pre-Celtic times from the Iberian peninsula.

The Greek historian Herodotus, writing about 440 B.C., provides us with an early account of blacks in Russia. He linked them to Egyptians and gave the following observations (translated by Aubrey de Selincourt) as proof:

> ... it is undoubtedly a fact that the Colchians are of Egyptian descent. I noticed this myself before I heard anyone else mention it, and when it occurred to me I asked some questions both in Colchis and in Egypt, and that the Colchians remembered the Egyptians more distinctly than the Egyptians remembered them. The Egyptians did, however, say that they thought the original Colchians were men from Sesostris' army. My own idea on the subject was based first on the fact that they have black skins and wooly hair (not that that accounts to much, as other natives have the same), and secondly, more especially, on the fact that the Colchians, the Egyptians, and the Ethiopians are the only races which from ancient times have practiced circumsicion... and now that I think of it, there is a further point of resemblance between the Colchians and the Egyptians: they share a method of weaving linen different from that of any other people; and there is also a similarity between them in language and way of living. The linen made in Colchis is known in Greece as Sardonian linen; that which comes from Egypt is called Egyptian.

Colchis was an ancient country bordering on the Black Sea in the western part of the Soviet Republic of Georgia known as Abkhazia; its official title is Abkhazian Autonomous Soviet Socialist Republic. Two other ancient scholars, Apollonios of Rhodes in *The Argonautica* and Diodorus in the *Library of History* agreed with Herodotus' assessment of the origins of the Colchians as remnants of the army of Senwosre (called by the Greeks Sesostris). He was a conquering black Egyptian king from the 12th dynasty (c.1900 B.C.) who led his armies into Asia.

Pindar of Thebes in his *Odes* described the swarthy features of the Colchians. Colchis was well known to the ancient Greeks. From at least the third century B.C., they knew it well enough to set a famous adventure story in that black land. It was to Colchis that Jason and the sailors of the ship Argo went in their quest for the Golden Fleece.

Today at Sukhumi, the capital of Abkhazia, there is still a small colony of blacks. In *Africans in Russia*, Lily Golden Hanga, the Russian born daughter of a white American mother and African American father, recounts the history of the region's African population. Not all of these individuals trace their ancestry back to the time of Senwosre. The Black Sea coast of Russia was the point of arrival for many African slaves from the time the area was part of the Turkish Ottoman Empire (c.1600s — 1810 A.D.).

A. Blakely, in *Russia and the Negro*, describes these Russian blacks and those in Yugoslavia and Iran. A. Burton, in his commentaries on Diodorus Siculus believed the present black residents of Abkhazia "... may well be the only Negro community in the Old World outside Africa and the Coastlands of the Indian Ocean.

In *The Glory of the Black Race*, Amr Ibn Bahr Al-Jahiz, an African Muslim savant from the ninth century A.D. described the global distributions of blacks:

> The Ethiopians, the Berbers, the Copts, the Zaghawa, the Moors, the people of Sindl, the Hindus, the Qamar, the Dabila,... and those beyond

them... the islands in the seas... are full up with Blacks from Hindustan to China.

On the Arabian peninsula and throughout Asia and the islands in the Pacific Ocean, ancient black civilizations once existed or in some cases, still exist. At Mada' in Salih in the Arabian Desert, is a mysterious rock city. In appearance, it resembles the carved rock city of Petra in Jordan where the final scenes of the movie "Indiana Jones and the Last Crusade" took place. Like Petra, Mada'in Salih is reached through a narrow passage leading into a cliff-bound valley.

Buildings were sculptured out of solid rock. Whole hillsides have been transformed into facades of temples, sanctuaries, even tombs with decorated pillars, capitals, and doorways. The buildings of Mada'in Salih also display carved birds and animals. This dusty, silent carved metropolis, now mostly in ruins, has water and was once a stop on a caravan route. Ibn Battuta claimed to have visited this ancient place about 1320 A.D. Even then the precise identity of its builders was a mystery. There is only one major clue to their

Figure 44

Map of the former Soviet Union showing the Abkhazskaya ASSR

possible appearance. On one of the building facades, cut away from the rock that surrounds it, is a carved representation of the head of a black man. His broad nose, thick lips, and high cheekbones, scowl out at the viewer defying anyone to solve the riddle of Mada'in Salih.

Could the figure represent the Nabateans, the supposed builders of the city? Some buildings carry Sabean inscriptions on them. Sabean was the written alphabet of the kingdom of Saba or Sheba. At its height, some historians believe its jurisdiction straddled the Red Sea extending from Ethiopia into Yemen and Saudi Arabia. Even so, the Sabean inscriptions are believed to have been made at Mada'in Salih long after the city was built.

In the area now occupied by Israel and Lebanon, scientists have found the remains of an African people called Natufians. They are believed to have travelled to Palestine from Nubia or northern Africa, perhaps four thousand years ago. Their skeletons, tools, and other remains tell us the Natufians were a remarkably skilled agricultural folk. They planted and harvested cereal grains and grasses.

Another interesting source for the widespread distribution of African people is the *Bible*. The "Table of Nations" presented in the tenth chapter of the Book of Genesis shows that the descendants of Ham went on to establish the kingdoms of Babylon, Phoenicia, Philistine, Sheba, and Egypt among others. The third century B.C. Babylonian historian Berosus reported that civilization was brought into southwest Asia by blacks. The Babylonian laws known as the Code of Hammurabi (c. 1700 B.C.) mentioned "the black faced race."

Ancient records and modern archeology inform us that the peoples of Sumer and Elam near the Persian Gulf were heavily mixed with blacks. The Sumerians called themselves "Sag-Gig" or black headed people, not black haired people. This suggests an African presence in the population, particularly in the leadership.

Blacks moved into the Indus Valley in prehistoric times. At the ruins of Mohenjo Daro and its sister city Harappa, evidence indicates that these cities traded with Arabia and East Africa thousands of years ago. Professor Runoko Rashidi, photo-historian Wayne Chandler, and others have documented the African contribution to the growth of civilization in the Indus Valley region around 2,000 B.C. The book "Black Presence In Early Asia" edited by Ivan Van Sertima examines various aspects of these contributions.

Classical writers clearly regarded the area stretching from Egypt to India as Ethiopia (meaning burnt face in Greek). Herodotus believed blacks from India were eastern Ethiopians and Africans were western Ethiopians.

Chinese archeologists have found the remains of blacks among the ruins of Shang dynasty structures in the Hwang Ho valley of eastern China. The Shang dynasty (1766–1022 B.C.) is considered to be among China's earliest ruling lines. Chinese histories from this period also mention blacks.

Beatrice J. Fleming and Marion J. Pryde, in *Distinguished Negroes Abroad*, a wide-ranging survey of black historical personalities around the globe, list the contributions of blacks to Asia:

> ...later explorations and investigations have proved that much of Asia's
> culture was borrowed from Africa. Religious rites, architectural features,

language patterns, and scientific formulae show influences of Africa. Travel between Asia and Africa was well established. Historians tell us that at one time Negroes were found in all of the countries of Southern Asia bordering the Indian Ocean and along the east coast as far as Japan. Consequently, interchange of ideas and customs flourished. Burial customs and monotheism were borrowed from Africa, the pyramid was based upon early African monuments; and poetry and literature carried many African words... In Asia as in other parts of the world, transplanted Africans made their contributions to the progress and culture of the countries.

An astounding demonstration of the ingenuity, skill, and bravery of these ancient black travellers is the story of their migration to the South Pacific. During the Stone Age, perhaps as long as 40,000 years ago, black peoples sailing from Africa or Asia populated a group of Pacific islands known today as Melanesia, a Greek term meaning "black islands." Melanesia, which includes Papua, New Guinea (so named by the Spanish sailor de Rete because of the population's similarities to blacks on the Guinea Coast of Africa), New Caledonia and Fiji is still home to blacks today. Blacks live in the northern Solomon Islands and the Bismarck Archipelago. Their ancient ancestors and those of the brown peoples of Micronesia ("little islands") and Polynesia ("many islands") crossed thousands of miles of open sea in flimsy wooden canoes without compasses, sextants, or maps.

For many years Europeans believed these peoples conducted their explorations and settlement by random chance or pure luck. During the European Age of Discovery, early white explorers were astonished to find so many of the Pacific islands inhabited by peoples seemingly without means of navigation. They saw them trade with distant islands but could not understand how these "primitives" could safely cross miles of open featureless ocean.

Spanish caravels and Portugese galleons quickly became lost without the navigational instruments the Arabs and Moors had brought them from the Orient. A Portuguese navigator, Pedro Fernandes de Quieros noted that even the most knowledgeable ship captains could "neither know nor determine their situation" without such instruments.

In the late 1960s, David Lewis spent nearly a year studying the traditional sailing methods of the peoples of the Pacific. He concluded that the islanders sailed exactly wherever they wanted to go. In We, the Navigators, Lewis pointed out that the islanders used stars to guide them to their destinations. They "sailed toward a star known to stand above their intended port of arrival. The islanders also made use of an "etak" or reference island in combination with the "star path." After one star had risen too high or had dipped beneath the horizon, the islanders guided themselves by another that ascended or descended in the same position. Traveling along one star path, Lewis and his master navigator, an old man named Tevake and his young friend Hippour tracked nine stars in a row to reach another island seventy miles away.

Lewis learned that these navigators had an intimate knowledge of the night sky, the specific appearance of neighboring islands, and a spiritual attachment to their watery highway with its currents, waves, and eddies. The travelling patterns of birds, fish, shapes and colors of clouds, even floating twigs could help take them safely to their objective even when they were momentarily lost. The knowledge was passed from father to son and held in strict confidence. Youth were trained on land and sea. Stones were used on land to replicate the position of stars. Keen eyesight and a superb memory enabled these seamen to voyage through sunlit waters as well as on overcast nights.

These ancient seamen invented the perfect craft for their travels. In Melanesia, the Ndrua or double canoe with two separate hulls of different lengths proved to be ideally suited for ocean travel. The black peoples of the South Pacific also developed the outrigger canoe, its framework extended outboard from the side of the canoe with its extra float providing stability. The "claw" sail usually, pitched at forty-five degrees to the masts was another innovation.

When the Phillipine volcano Mount Pinatubo began erupting in the summer of 1991, it helped reveal the existence of a group of blacks living on those islands. The mudslides, clouds of ash, and showers of pumice fell on the ancestral lands of the Aeta. Short, with black skins and wooly hair, the Aeta of the Phillipines are part of a group of Africoid peoples called Negritos also inhabiting Malaya and the Andaman islands.

Environmental catastrophies associated with the eruption of Mount Pinatubo which the Aeta call "grandfather" have dislodged them from their aboriginal homes in the mountainous jungles of the northern Phillipines and forced them to seek havens among the general Phillipine population. Their future is uncertain. During 1991, Mount Pinatubo hurled nearly 30 million tons of rocks, gas, and ash into the upper atmosphere in what is believed to be the twentieth century's most violent sequence of volcanic explosions. Pinatubo unleashed a dust cloud that winds are carrying around the world today.

Australian Aborigines tend not to be scientifically classified as blacks by many European scientists because even though they have Africoid features and black skins, many lack woolly hair. Yet, we know that the Aborigines were on the leading edge of the great wave of black travellers sweeping out of Africa and Asia to populate the Pacific islands forty thousand years ago. Like some African ethnic groups, Aborigines attach mystical importance to imprinting images of their hands on cave or cliff walls. Many of the handprints found in Australia and Africa show mutilated or disfigured fingers above the main knuckle. The stenciled method of hand imprinting appears to be the same whether it is among the San (Bushmen) of South Africa or the Aborigines of Australia. It is worth noting that boomerangs, from the Australian Aborigine word "bumarin," were made not only in Australia, but in Egypt, Europe, India, and prehistoric America.

In *Lost Cities and Ancient Mysteries of Africa and Arabia*, David Hatcher Childress puts forth his belief that blacks are not originally from Africa. They sailed to Africa, he claims, from Central America or Mexico. He points to a variety of evidence including huge old stone carvings and small figurines with African features to explain his position. He is supported to some extent by James Churchward and his book *Children of Mu*.

Most scholars disagree with these views. Several have noted, however, the great antiquity of black presence in Mexico. Mexican ethnologist Nicolas Leon believed that blacks "were the first inhabitants of Mexico." Leon was struck by the recurrence of black themes and figures in the country's oldest traditions. He believed that the remaining unmixed Africans died in wars with the Spanish conquistadores.

Peter DeRoo, in the *History of America Before Columbus*, mentioned the existence of several ancient black groups in the Americas:

> there were many, as we may see in Rafinesque's *Account of The Ancient Nations of America*. Such are the Charruas of Brazil, the black Carabees of St. Vincent in the Gulf of Mexico, the Jamassi of Florida, the dark complexioned Californians who are perhaps the dark men mentioned in the Quiche traditions and by some old Spanish adventurers. Such, again, is the tribe of which Balboa saw some representatives in his passage of the Isthmus of Darien in the year 1513. It would seem from the expressions made use of by Gomara that these were Negroes.

DeRoo also quotes John T. Short, author of *The North Americans of Antiquity*, published in New York in 1880, on similarities between African and American languages:

> "it is worthy of note that several eminent scholars have observed the remarkable similarity of grammatical structure between the Central American and certain transatlantic languages, especially the Basque in some of the languages of western Africa."

Africans have literally circled the globe exploring and settling from humankind earliest times as Gerald Massey has stated in *Ancient Egypt, The Light of the World*:

> The one sole race that can be traced among the aborigines all over the earth or below, is the dark race of a dwarf negrito type.

THE ERA OF MODERN EXPLORATIONS

In more recent times blacks have journeyed around the world into some of its remotest regions alone or accompanied by others. In September 1519, at least three blacks: Anton Moreno, "Juan, a Negro," and an unnamed black servant of Juan Carvalho, accompanied Ferdinand Magellan when he sailed around the world. Daniel Hawthorne, author of *Ferdinand Magellan*, writes that the Magellan's five-ship fleet had "... several Moors, two or three Negroes..." J.A. Rogers also notes the existence of Moorish crewmen and names three men definitely listed as Negroes, though one name is different from names I found. The exact names of crewmen is in doubt. Historians generally place the total number of crewmen between 237 and 280 boys and men.

Magellan's voyage began at Seville in Spain. He steered for the Canary Islands and then slid down the coast of Africa as far as the Cape Verde Islands. From there he crossed the Atlantic, sailing to Brazil.

Coasting down the eastern side of South America, Magellan's fleet stopped often to trade with the Indians. South of Brazil, he saw a large peak near the mouth of the Rio de la Plata River. He named the area "Monte Video" which means I see a mountain. Montevideo is the name of the capitol of what is now the country of Uruguay. Later, Magellan saw tall, painted, naked men wearing shoes stuffed with straw. He labelled that region of South America "Patagonia" or land of the big-footed ones.

By this time, Magellan had sailed off his maps. It was winter and his men did not know it as they navigated the South American straits now named for their "Captain General" but they were moving toward the South Pole. They saw creatures they called "Patos sin altos" or ducks without wings — penguins. The crew was frightened and hungry. When Magellan finally rounded South America and entered the Pacific Ocean, he had put down a mutiny, marooned the ringleaders, and seen one of his ships turn back.

In the Pacific, Magellan was killed in a fight with Phillipine warriors on the Island of Mocatan. In 1523, the "Victoria," the only one of Magellan's ships still seaworthy, finally saw the landfall of the Spanish coast. Under the command of Captain Juan Sebastian d'Elcano, with a crew of seventeen survivors, the world had been circled.

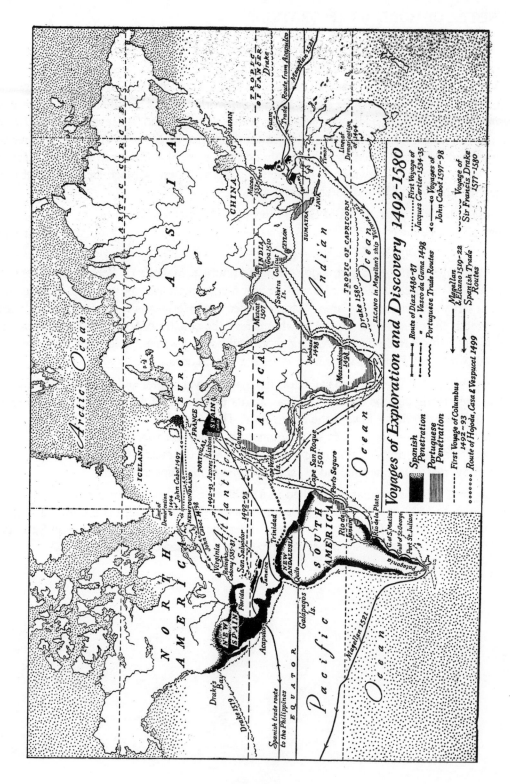

Figure 45

Major European voyages of exploration to America, 1492–1580

GUSTAVUS VASSA

OR

Olaudah Equiano

A NATIVE AFRICAN FROM THE COAST OF GUINEA

Figure 46

Olaudah Equiano, also called Gustavus Vassa

TOWARD THE POLES

Matthew Henson was not the first black explorer to head for the polar regions. The earliest black man to sail to the regions near the North Pole is better known as an autobiographer, abolitionist, merchant seaman, and religious missionary. His *Interesting Narrative* has been hailed as a classic of English and African American literature. His name was Olaudah Equiano.

His autobiography describing his being kidnapped into slavery from his home in what is now Nigeria, surviving the horrendous Middle Passage, living as a slave, and gaining his freedom went through eight British editions and one American edition during his lifetime. It is now required reading in many schools and colleges throughout the United States.

Little notice is taken of Equiano's role as an explorer and his journey to the Arctic in 1772 with C.J. Phipps aboard the vessel "Race Horse." This is how Equiano described the voyage:

> I was roused by the sound of fame to seek new adventures, to find, towards the North Pole, what our Creator never intended we should, a passage to India. An expedition was fitting out to explore a north-east passage, conducted by the Honorable Constantine John Phipps, since Lord Mulgrave, in his Majesty's sloop of war the Race Horse...

> On the 4th of June we sailed towards our destined place, the Pole; and on the 15th of the same month we were off Shetland.

[Equiano describes how, while trying to write in his journal below deck, he accidentally set fire to himself and the ship. The flames were quickly put out. Equiano was reprimanded. He returned to his assigned task.]

> On the 20th of June we began to use Dr. Irving's apparatus for making salt water fresh. I used to attend the distillery; I frequently purified from twenty-six to forty gallons a day. The water thus distilled was perfectly pure, well tasted, and free from salt; and was used on various occasions on board the ship. On the 28th of June, being in lat 78° we made Greenland, where I was surprised to see the sun did not set. The weather now became extremely cold; and as we sailed between north and east, which was our course, we saw many very high and curious mountains of ice; and also a great number of very large whales, which used to come close to our ship, and blow the water up to a very great height in the air. One morning we had vast quantities of sea-horses about the ship, which neighed exactly like any other horses. We fired some harpoon guns amongst them in order to take some, but we could not get any.

> On the 30th, the Captain of a Greenland ship came on board, and told us of three ships that were lost in the ice; however, we still held on our course till July the 11th, when we were stopped by one compact impenetrable body of ice. We ran along it from east to west above ten degrees; and on the 27th we got as far north as 80°, 37'; and in 19 or 20 degrees east longitude from London. On the 29th and 30th of July, we

saw one continued plain of smooth unbroken ice bounded only by the horizon, and we fastened to a piece of ice that was eight yards eleven inches thick. We had generally sunshine, and constant day-light; which gave cheerfulness and novelty to the whole of this striking, grand, and uncommon scene; and, to heighten it still more, the reflection of the sun from the ice gave the clouds a most beautiful appearance.

We remained hereabouts until the 1st of August, when the two ships got completely fastened in the ice occasioned by the loose ice that set in from the sea. This made our situation very dreadful and alarming; so that on the 7th day we were in very great apprehension of having the ship squeezed to pieces.

[The ice pack loosened after eleven days allowing the ships to free themselves and return to England. Equiano sums up his adventure]

And thus ended our Arctic voyage, to the no small joy of all on board, after having been absent four months, in which time, at the imminent hazard of our lives, we explored nearly as far towards the Pole as 81 degrees north, and 20 degrees east longitude; being much farther, by all accounts, than any navigator had ever ventured before; in which we fully proved the impracticability of finding a passage that way to India.

Paul Belloni du Chaillu, the African explorer, ventured into Scandinavia shortly before his death to investigate the origins of the English people. He criss-crossed Sweden, Norway, Lapland, Finland, and Russia. In 1889, he produced *The Viking Age* in two volumes, which he called "the early history, manners, and customs of the ancestors of the English speaking nations." Prior to that he had authored *Land of the Midnight Sun* on a similar theme. Du Chaillu is believed to be the originator of the phrases "Land of the Midnight Sun" and "Land of the Long Night."

The most famous black explorer is probably Matthew Henson, the co-discoverer of the North Pole. While accounts of Henson's early years vary, they agree that he was born in Charles County, Maryland and lived with an uncle in Washington, D.C. While there received his early education.

Henson became a seaman, and later worked as a longshoreman, bellhop, laborer, and coachman. In 1887, he met Peary and served as his valet on a trip to Nicaragua. In the jungle, Peary learned to count on Henson's navigational skills and the knowledge he had acquired through a sailing career and time spent in many different ports.

In 1891, Henson went with Peary to the arctic for the first time. Counting their final trip in 1908-1909, Peary and Henson went to the polar regions six times. On the final trip, Peary, Henson, five white assistants and several Eskimos set out from Cape Columbia on Ellesmere Island off the coast of Greenland. The trip over the ice was brutal. The special sled Henson designed for the trip was subjected to a grueling test by men, dogs, and the elements. Peary became ill.

One hundred thirty three miles from the pole, Peary sent the last of his five white assistants back. There were six men on the final leg of the race for the pole; Peary, Henson, and four Eskimos. Peary was too weak to maintain the pace needed to get to the pole in the shortest time. On April 6, 1909, Henson forged ahead with three of the Eskimos leav-

Figure 47
Matthew Henson

ing Peary about forty five minutes behind. Henson and four Eskimos reached the Pole first. The weakened Peary joined them later.

In his book, *A Negro Explorer At the North Pole*, Henson, with modesty and deference, described his feelings as he raised the U.S. flag at the pole:

> As it snapped and crackled with the wind, I felt a savage joy and exulta- tion. Another world's accomplishment was done and finished, and as in the past, from the beginning of history, wherever the world's work was done by a white man, he had been accompanied by a colored man. From the building of the pyramids and the journey to the Cross, to the discovery of the North pole, the Negro had been the faithful and constant com- panion of the Caucasian, and I felt all that it was possible for me to feel, that it was I, a lowly member of my race, who had been chosen by fate to represent it, at this, almost the last of the world's great work.

One of the men Peary sent back, Donald MacMillan, later recalled "Henson, the colored man went with Peary because he was a better man than any of his white assis- tants." He confirmed rumors that Peary's illness had made him late arriving at the North Pole after Henson. MacMillan told Lowell Thomas it was Henson who placed the Stars and Stripes at the top of the world.

Peary asked Henson not to speak publicly about the events at the Pole. Most newspaper accounts omitted Henson. The friendship the two men had shared for twenty years ended. Twenty eight years after the dash to the North Pole, Henson was made a member of the Explorers Club. He died in 1955.

Henson's exploits inspired the career of Dr. Herbert L. Frisby, another black arctic ex- plorer. Frisby was the second black man to arrive at the North Pole (1956). A science teacher and school principal in Baltimore, Maryland, Frisby performed extensive research on Eskimo culture and on Henson's true role in the discovery of the North pole. Frisby was the first to prove that Henson arrived at the Pole before Peary.

Frisby made over twenty trips to the arctic regions. Traveling during World War II as a correspondent for the Afro-American Newspaper chain, Frisby covered black troops sta- tioned in northern Alaska, Canada, and Greenland. Frisby converted his home into a Hen- son museum and was responsible for the passage of a bill through the Maryland State Legislature installing a bronze plaque in honor of Henson at the State House in Annapolis.

Henson also stirred the imagination of Dr. Allen Counter, another black explorer. Counter established himself as an explorer and ethnologist studying African bush people in the tropical forests of South America. He chronicled his explorations in the book, *I Sought My Brother*. In 1986, he journeyed to Greenland and located the Eskimo sons of Peary and Henson. With great effort he was able to fulfill the wish of Ahnahkaq Henson, to meet his father's family in Maryland. Counters' book, *North Pole Legacy; Black, White, and Eskimo*, describes the entire story.

On August 3, 1958 when the submarine "Nautilus" became the first ship to sail under the north polar ice pack, two black sailors were part of the crew. The sub began its under- water cruise at Point Barrow in Alaska and surfaced in the Greenland Sea.

Darryl Roberts is another black Arctic explorer. In 1989, not far from where Peary and

Figure 48

Some of Matthew Henson's Black and Inuit relatives

Figure 49

Dr. Herbert M. Frisby

Henson set out for the North Pole eighty years earlier, Roberts and seven other men began a 56-day walk to the Pole. Roberts was the first American and youngest person ever to trek from Canada to the North Pole. He was part of an international team that began their mission on March 20, 1989 to bring media attention to the ways in which pollution damages the ozone layer.

Traveling through frozen wastes where the temperature dropped to 75 degrees below zero and winds up to 40 miles per hour flung ice crystals fast enough to cut his face, Roberts suffered frostbite and lost part of his heel. He refused to be airlifted back to the base camp. He kept up his strength with protein biscuits, whale meat, and butter. His desire to do something different took him from his birthplace in Harlem and a job as an Outward Bound instructor to the Pole. After his return to the states, he began a lecture tour of schools across the country. His message is based upon what he learned on his walk to the Pole: "I proved to myself something that I always suspected to be true: a person who wants a thing badly enough will do whatever is necessary to get it." Roberts tells his young audiences that he wants to share his experience "with anyone who is willing to use it as an example to make their dreams come true."

Black explorers have also ventured to the South Pole. In 1820, when Nathanial Palmer explored what is now Palmers Land, a southern section of the Antarctic Peninsula, he had a black crewman named Peter Harvey aboard his ship "Hero." The 31 year old Harvey was born in Philadelphia, Pennsylvania. Several years later, the ship Huron, like many others, approached the South polar ice pack but did not enter. On board were three blacks, Cato Tobias and an unnamed cook and steward.

James B. De Saule was a member of the first U.S. Government Scientific Expedition to survey and explore the Pacific Ocean and South Seas. Under the command of Lieutenant Charles Wilkes, the expedition embarked from Norfolk, Virginia in 1838. De Saule was aboard the 650-ton ship "Peacock." Over 300 men in six ships comprised the expedition. The ships cruised down to South America and around Cape Horn. They crossed the Pacific taking soundings and making nautical charts. After visiting Australia and New Zealand, the fleet sailed toward the South Pole.

In early January 1840, the "Peacock" was separated from the rest of the fleet during a storm. On January 16, 1840, the same day the "Peacock" rejoined the fleet, its lookouts sighted the Antarctic ice pack. The ships worked their way past huge icebergs. An ice floe damaged the "Peacock's" rudder and nearly sheared the ship's bow. The crew headed her back to Australia for repairs. Hastily refitted, the Peacock sailed back to duty with the fleet. Wilke's tiny fleet cruised along the continental ice shelf for 1,500 miles.

In July 1841, the ship finally ran aground at the mouth of the Columbia River, off the West coast of the United States-Canadian border. The crew was stranded. DeSaule was among the last to be rescued. The rest of the United States Exploring Expedition returned to New York in June 1842. The expedition was the first to announce the existence of the Continent of Antarctica.

According to J.A. Rogers in *Africa's Gifts to America*, one black may have accompanied Admiral Richard E. Byrd on one of his last two Antarctic explorations. These were Operation High Jump and Operation Deep Freeze, which explored and mapped hundreds of thousands of square miles of Antarctic territory, which were major undertakings. High

Jump, for example, (1946-1947), used 13 ships and 4,700 men. Operation Deep Freeze occurred during the 1950s.

Figure 50

Inuit igloos

Figure 51

Arctic navigation

CHAPTER 5

EXPLORING NEW HORIZONS

The Ethiopians were the first who invented the science of stars, and gave names to the planets, not at random and without meaning, but descriptive of the qualities which they conceived them to possess; and it was from them that this art passed, still in an imperfect state, to the Egyptians.

De Astrologia 3

The link between blacks and the stars was already old when Lucian, the second century B.C. Greek satirist and wit, wrote those lines. He went on to describe the Ethiopian's love of learning and the high regard they held for wisdom noting these Africans as "being in all else wiser than other men." The Greeks named three constellations of stars after an Ethiopian royal family from their mythology: Cepheus a king, his wife Queen Cassiopeia, and their daughter, Andromeda.

Prehistoric Africans observed the stars in minute detail adding them to their own unique cosmologies. They gave the stars the characteristics of men or animals as they watched them make their way across the night skies. Later, as myths and legends, beliefs and observations translated themselves into religion or science, the study of the stars branched in two major directions — astrology and astronomy. Both have some of their earliest manifestations in Africa.

Although mainstream Egyptologists disagree, a strong argument can be made for the use of the Great Pyramid in Egypt as an astronomical observatory. There is a reference to such a function, found by Richard Proctor, an English astronomer, in the writings of Proclus, (410–485 A.D.) a Greek philosopher. His critique of Plato's *Timaeus* described the top of the structure as a platform for ancient astronomers prior to the setting of the capstone.

In 1883, Proctor published *The Great Pyramid: Observatory, Tomb and Temple.* He theorized that the Great Pyramid served as an astronomical observatory as each step in its construction took it higher into the sky. The most extraordinary part of his book lay in his suggestion that the grand gallery of the Great Pyramid, a one hundred fifty-seven foot long, thirty foot high ascending passage of no use in a simple tomb, was really an observation platform before the top of the pyramid was encased in stone. Proctor described how features still visible on the walls today would have allowed ancient priest-astronomers to track the movements of stars.

The Great Pyramid and the towering colonnade of the temple of Amun-Ra at Karnak are among the many ancient Egyptian temples and tombs oriented toward the sun or the stars. The Great Pyramid's measurements contain a value for pi and the basic dimensions of the "golden section." The measurements of the king's chamber reveal the geometric constant: $A^2 + B^2 = C^2$.

According to C.R. Gibbs in *The Afro-American Inventor*:

> The first calendar in Egypt began with the earliest recorded date, 4241 B.C. Egyptian star charts occur as early as 3500 B.C.; early indicative of a systematic study of astronomy.
>
> The Egyptians were cognizant of the fact that Mercury and Venus were closer to the sun than were the Earth, Mars, Jupiter, and Saturn. To aid

them in their astral observations the Egyptians invented the Merkhet. This device, consisting of a forked stick and plumb line, was used as an aid in star mapping.

The Egyptian priests, the ancient guardians and accumulators of knowledge, told Herodotus in the fifth century B.C. that the sun had not risen where it rose then.

This implied that they kept records of the procession of equinoxes, covering at least 26,000 years. The Greek historian, Diogenes Laertius (3rd century A.D.) claimed that astronomical records of Egyptian priests began in 49,219 B.C. He also told of a register of 373 solar and 832 lunar eclipses, which would cover a period of 10,000 years.

The lunar calendar of Babylon and the solar calendar of Egypt coincided in the year 11,542 B.C. The calendrical computations of India began with the year 11,652 B.C. According to Plato, North African priests fixed the date for the sinking of Atlantis at 9850 B.C. Even though those dates can be questioned we can see that the ancients were closer to the truth than many of the scholars of later eras.

Additional evidence of the ancient Egyptian knowledge of the stars can be determined through an examination of their beliefs in astrology, the ways in which heavenly bodies influence human events. The temple of Hathor at Dendera, north of Luxor, was not only the final destination for the sick and lame in search of miracle cures, its aisles, vestibules and ceilings are filled with astrological and astronomical allusions and symbols. In the eastern rooftop chapel is a copy of the only circular zodiac in Egypt. The original was removed from the temple by Napoleon's troops and placed in the Louvre in Paris.

Believed to be influenced by Babylonians and Greeks, the circular zodiac still reveals a surprising knowledge of the heavens and is firmly in keeping with the star knowledge revealed throughout the rest of the temple. Symbolic representatives of the solstices, the rotation of the earth and the shape of the universe appear on the walls of the temple.

The temple of Hathor at Dendera was designed and built during the Greek occupation of Egypt by African architects and labor and administered by African priests. The temple's building materials incorporated stones from earlier temples on that site. Given that the Greeks conquered Egypt (c.330 B.C.) near the end of its greatness it is unfortunate that this relatively young structure does not reveal more about its historical and architectural antecedents.

The temple complex at Karnak, the temple of Osiris at Abydos, and the temple of Isis at Philae provide some other examples of the precision and reverence with which the ancient places of worship were chosen, the stars to which they were aligned, how they were constructed, and the artistry with which they were decorated.

In addition, to astronomy and astrology, the ancient Egyptians had an interest in flight. In 1969, Dr. Khalil Messiah found a model glider in a storeroom of the Cairo Museum. First excavated in 1898, the tiny glider is aerodynamically balanced and has a tail rudder.

The Garstang-Sayce expedition of 1906-1907 found among the ruins of Meroe, one of the capitals of ancient Kush, a drawing that mystified them. Drawn in firm strokes, the picture shows a pair of men guiding a huge object that resembles an antenna or telescope. Traditional archeologists dismiss this interpretation but the picture hints at a high level of scientific sophistication during the height of the Kushite empire. A copy of the drawing is published in *Curse of the Pharaohs* by Philipp Vandenburg. Until the Kushite script is deciphered, however, the exact function of this machine cannot be known and the exact level of Kushite science cannot be fairly evaluated.

Modern knowledge of Kushite science has also suffered from the Egypt-centered biases of traditional Egyptologists and their continuing efforts to attribute every Kushite advance to an Egyptian source. Kushite scientists were able to determine the level of the Nile's yearly flood and attribute it to the amount of rainfall at its headwaters, while the Egyptians still believed in a metaphysical cause.

Kush, in Nubia, was a power on the world stage from the eighth century B.C., when it conquered Egypt from Elephantine to the marshes of the Nile delta, until the third century A.D. These black pharaohs and queens presided over a physical and spiritual rebirth of Egyptian values and forms of expression. The strength and character of its leaders found mention in the Hebrew Bible and the writings of Greek and Roman historians.

Pyramid building and iron smelting were the hallmarks of Kushite civilization which itself was far more flexible, adaptive and inquisitive than is generally recognized. Kushite trade with the interior of Africa, Egypt, Greece, and India is reflected in design motifs, religious practices, and objects of commerce. The writings of Drusilla Houston, W.E.B. DuBois, and Bruce Williams among others point to a Nubian civilization that antedated and nourished that of ancient Egypt.

The kingdom of Kush finally fell to the forces of King Ezana of Axum in the fourth century A.D. Axum or Aksun comprised much of what is now Ethiopia. Here too, are some fascinating references not only to astronomy but also to space travel.

In the *Kebra Negast* (Glory of Kings), the national mytho-historical chronicles of Ethiopia, translated in 1932 by Sir E.A. Wallis Budge, there is mention of a "heavenly car." According to the chronicle, King Solomon seduced Makeda, the Queen of Sheba. They fell in love. After she returned to her kingdom, she gave birth to their son, Menelik. Solomon went to see his son in some sort of flying vehicle. "The king... and all who obeyed his word, flew on the wagon without pain and suffering, and without sweat or exhaustion, and traveled in one day a distance which took three months to traverse (on foot)."

Ethiopia contains many other wonders: the monolithic rock churches of King Lalibela carved out of mountains nine hundred years ago, huge stone obelisks, the stone pylons of Tuja, and the drawings at Chabbe Ravine testify to high science lost long ago.

In Kenya, there are two astronomical observatories dating back to three hundred years before the birth of Christ. Like some smaller African versions of Stonehenge, these two sites contain stones oriented towards stars far above the earth. Of the two sites, Namoratunga II has greater astronomical significance. The site appears to have functioned as a kind of astronomical calendar on which the local peoples based a year of 12 months divided into three hundred fifty-four days. The stone pillars at Namoratunga II were aligned to various stars or constellations including Sirius, Aldebaran, the Pleiades, and Central Orion.

Originally reported in *Science* magazine (May 19, 1978) and again in *Blacks In Science, Ancient and Modern*, the astronomical sites in Kenya provide insight into the scientific accomplishments of early African peoples, an aspect of black studies often ignored by historians.

Celestial observations were not confined to Africans on the eastern coast of the continent. The Dogon people of Mali in West Africa have a seven hundred year tradition of astronomy. The Dogon and their culture were the subjects of an intense twenty five year study by two French scientists, Marcel Griaule and Germaine Dieterlen. The Frenchmen published their work in a book entitled *The Pale Fox*. The book reported that the Dogon observed four of Jupiter's moons, several spiral galaxies, the Sirius star cluster, and the rings of Saturn with the unaided eye. Not only did they observe and teach the movements of these celestial bodies, they correctly described the surface and orbit of the moon, the density of Sirius B, and the structure of the Milky Way galaxy of which the earth is a part.

In addition to the Dogon tradition of star gazing, their cultural and linguistic neighbors, the Bozo, the Bambara, and the Minianka also practice astronomy. Some experts have speculated that their ethnic groups learned astronomy from the Egyptians. And, there is evidence that the Bozo, for example, had contact with pharaonic-era Egyptians.

African interest in astronomy, astrology and even flight it seems did not begin with their initial contacts with Europeans. The interest already existed manifesting itself through religion, history, and the physical sciences. That same interest, part of an ageless continuum, shows itself in the presence of black astronaut-explorers supported by the efforts of dozens of black scientists, researchers, physicians, technical specialists, pilots, and inventors. In the 1940s, the black scientist Dr. Clarence Reed White urged manned space exploration.

During the same period, "Tex Johnston" became a test pilot on some of this nation's earliest jet planes. At Bell Aircraft, he tested the XP-59, the first U.S. jet fighter. Along with white pilots like Chuck Yeager, Johnston broke the sound barrier in the XS-1 Rocket. He joined the Boeing Company and test flew the XB-47, the first six-engine jet bomber; and the XB-52 (now the B-52) Bomber. Johnston's daring career is the subject of the biography *Tex Johnston, Jet-Age Test Pilot*.

Another early black contributor to the American space program was Adolphus Samms, a sergeant in the U.S. Army. His career is reviewed in *The Afro-American Inventor* by C.R. Gibbs:

> The space age began on October 4, 1957. On that date Russia launched Sputnik I, the first artificial satellite to circle the earth.
>
> The United States somewhat taken by surprise, geared itself to the task of catching up to the Soviet Union.
>
> This necessitated an immense astral mobilization program. With the various government agencies participating, guidance and propulsion systems, rocketry, communications, men, machines and the retrieval of these items all had to be quickly considered.
>
> Against this backdrop of planning and preparation, Adolphus Samms patented his first invention — a parachute release mechanism.

This invention patented on July 29, 1958, has since been modified for use in recovering objects of military importance and by some civilian air transportation companies.

Sergeant Samms, while stationed at the U.S. Weapons Test Station in Yuma, Arizona produced other products still more closely allied with the space program. Four months after Alan B. Shepard made his 15-minute space flight and five months after Yuri Gagarin became the first man to circle the earth in a space ship — Adolphus Samms patented his rocket engine pump feed system. This system patented in September 1961, aided the flow of liquid fuel or solid fuel to rocket engines.

The same year John Glenn became the first American to circle the Earth, Samms patented his most ambitious project — an air frame center support. This apparatus eliminated the second and third stage engines from multistage rockets, thus stripping the vehicle of dead weight and also facilitating greater possible payloads. In 1965 Sergeant Samms patented a multiple stage rocket and an air breathing booster. As the "soaring sixties" drew to a close, ideas continued to pour forth from the mind of this black serviceman. On June 21, 1966 he patented an emergency release for extraction chute mechanism and in March of 1967 a rocket motor fuel feed system.

His work has been commended by NASA and the President's Office of Science and Technology.

Sergeant Samms' patents are on file at the Pentagon.

In 1980, the first of a new breed of black explorers blasted off into space. This is a copy of the dispatch the Associated Press placed on its wires:

MOSCOW, Sept. 18 (AP) — A Cuban cosmonaut and a Soviet mission commander rocketed into space tonight aboard the Soyuz 38 spaceship, the Soviet news agency Tass reported.

The Cuban cosmonaut, Arnaldo Tamayo Mendez, is the seventh non-Soviet citizen to fly in the Soviet Union's Intercosmos space program. Tamayo Mendez, whose photograph shown on Moscow television suggested he was of mixed black and caucasian origin, is 38.

He and his Soviet mission commander, space veteran Yuri V. Romanenko, are to link up with the Soviet Salyut space station, where two Soviet cosmonauts are within two weeks of breaking a space endurance record.

Mendez and Romanenko spent a week aboard the Salyut 6 orbiting laboratory. They performed twenty scientific experiments. They undocked their spaceship and returned safely to earth on September 26, 1980.

The 1970s saw four black astronauts in the American space shuttle program with others to follow.

The presence of African American astronauts was the result of tremendous effort, preparation, and perseverance. In 1963, U.S. Air Force Captain Edward J. Dwight, Jr.,

Charles F. Bolden, Jr.

Frederick D. Gregory

Guion S. Bluford, Jr.

Mae C. Jemison

Figure 52

Current African American astronauts

was the first black man chosen for the American astronaut training program. Dwight encountered passive institutional resistance and outright racism from the beginning of his training. He publicly criticized the Air Force and was not selected to continue the astronaut training program.

Four years later, another black Air Force officer, Major Robert Henry Lawrence, completed the astronaut program. Born in Chicago, Lawrence was a jet pilot and held a doctorate in nuclear chemistry. Officially an astronaut designee, he was killed in a jet crash in June of 1967. Lawrence and his achievements remain generally unknown. He was about to be assigned to the Air Force manned orbiting laboratory project. Lawrence was the first black astronaut and the ninth astronaut to be killed in an accident.

Lieutenant Colonel Guy Bluford was the first African American in space. Nearly three years after Mendez, Bluford went into space aboard the shuttle "Challenger." He took part in various medical tests and helped place the Indian national Satellite, INSAT-1B in orbit from the shuttle's cargo bay.

By the mid-1980s along with Bluford were black astronauts Colonel Frederick C. Gregory, Colonel Charles F. Bolden, Jr., and Ronald E. McNair. McNair, formerly a staff physicist with Hughes Research Laboratories, was the first black astronaut to lose his life during a mission. He was one of seven astronauts to die in the explosion of the "Challenger" space shuttle in 1986.

Since the Challenger explosion, only one African American has been selected for astronaut training. She is Mae C. Jemison, the first black female. She was one of 15 astronaut candidates selected from 1,900 applicants. A medical doctor, Jemison also holds a degree in chemical engineering from Stanford University and has completed requirements for a degree in African and Afro-American Studies. A medical researcher with an engineering background, Jemison has been a Peace Corps Medical Officer in West Africa and served as a medical researcher, curriculum development expert, and general medical practitioner. She is one of three astronauts scheduled for a mission to be conducted sometime in 1992.

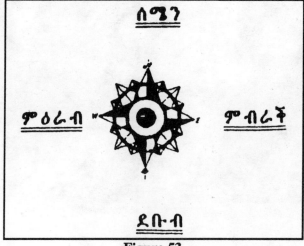

Figure 53

Ethiopian compass

BIBLIOGRAPHY
Selected Bibliography

Books

Ajayi, Ade J.F. and Ian Espie. A Thousand Years of West African History. Ibadan: Ibadan University Press, 1965.

Aldred, Cyril. The Egyptians. New York: Thames and Hudson, Inc., 1987.

Anderson, Benjamin. Narrative of a Journey to Musardu. New York: S.W. Green, 1870.

_____. Narrative of the Expedition Dispatched to Mugahdu. Monrovia, Liberia: College of West Africa Press, 1902.

Athearn, Robert G. The New World Volume I. New York: Choice Publishing, Inc., 1988.

Beasley, Delilah L. The Negro Trail Blazers of California. Los Angeles: NP, 1919.

Bernal, Martin. Black Athena, Volume II. New Brunswick: Rutgers University Press, 1991.

Billard, Jules B. (ed.). Ancient Egypt Discovering Its Splendors. Washington, DC: National Geographic Society, 1978.

Blake, H.O. The History of Slavery and the Slave Trade. Columbus, Ohio: H. Miller, 1860.

Brame, Herman L. The World Records of Black People. Portland: Sudan Publications, 1983.

Brendon, J.A. Great Navigators and Discoverers. Freeport, New York: Books for Libraries Press, 1967.

Brooks, Lester. Great Civilizations of Ancient Africa. New York: Four Winds Press, 1971.

Bunbury E.H. A History of Ancient Geography. New York: Dover Publications, Inc., 1959.

Burkholder, Mark A. and Lyman L. Johnson. Colonial Latin America. New York: Oxford University Press, 1990.

Calkins, Carroll E., ed. The Story of America. Pleasantville, New York: The Readers Digest Association, Inc., 1975.

Campbell, Robert. A Pilgrimage to My Motherland. New York: Thomas Hamilton, 1861.

Cantor, Gorge. Historic Black Landmarks. Detroit: Visible Ink, 1990.

Carpenter, Rhys. Beyond the Pillars of Hercules. New York: Delacorte Press, 1966.

Cary, M. and E.H. Warmington. The Ancient Explorers. New York: Dodd, Mead and Company, 1929.

Childress, David Hatcher. Lost Cities and Ancient Mysteries of Africa and Arabia. Stelle, Illinois: Adventures Unlimited Press, 1989.

Clark, J.C. A History of Texas. Boston: D.C. Heath and Company, 1940.

Clark, John Henrick (ed.) with Amy Jacques Garvey. Marcus Garvey and the Vision of Africa. New York: Vintage Books, 1974.

Day, Alan Edwin. Discovery and Exploration a Reference Handbook. New York: K.G. Saur Clive Bingley, 1980.

Daniel, Hawthorne. Ferdinand Magellan. New York: Double Day, 1964.

Diop, Cheik Anta. Civilization or Barbarism. Brooklyn, New York: Lawrence Hill, 1991.

deGraft-Johnson, J.C. African Glory. Baltimore: Black Classics Press, 1986.

Delany, Martin R. Official Report of the Niger Valley Exploring Party. New York: Thomas Hamilton, 1861.

Desroches-Noblecourt, Christine. Tutankhamen Life and Death of a Pharaoh. Boston: New York Graphic Society, 1978.

Du Chaillu, Paul B. Explorations and Discoveries In Equatorial Africa. London: John Murray, 1861.

Ellis, George Washington. Negro Culture in West Africa. New York: The Neale Publishing Company, 1914.

Equiano, Olaudah. The Interesting Narrative of the Life of Olandah Equiano. Leeds: James Nichols, 1814.

Evans, Ivor, ed. Brewer's Dictionary of Phrase and Fable. New York: Harper and Row, 1970.

Fell, Barry. America B.C. New York: Pocket Books, 1989.

Fishel, Jr., Leslie H. and Benjamin Quarles. The Black American: A Documentary History. Glenview, Illinois: Scott, Foresman and Company, 1970.

Fleming, Beatrice Jackson and Marion Jackson Pryde. Distinguished Negroes Abroad. Washington, DC: The Associated Publishers, 1988.

Franklin, John Hope. From Slavery to Freedom, Third Edition. New York: Vintage Books, 1969.

Garlake, Peter. The Kingdoms of Africa. New York: Peter Bedrick Books, 1990.

Goetzmann, William H. Army Exploration In the American West 1803-1863. Lincoln: University of Nebraska Press, 1979.

_____. Exploration And Empire. New York: W.W. Norton, 1978.

Gibbs, C.R. The Afro-American Inventor. NP. Washington, DC, 1975.

Hardesty, Von and Dominick Pisano. Black Wings. Washington, DC: National Air and Space Museum, 1983.

Hartwig, G. The Polar and Tropical Worlds: A Description of Man and Nature. Chicago: C.A. Nichols, 1874.

Hermann, Paul. Conquest By Man. New York: Harper and Brothers, 1954.

Herodotos, Herodotus: The Histories, A. de Selincourt, Trans. London's Penguin, 1954.

History of the United States. New York: Charles Wiley, 1825.

Jackson, John G. Ages of Gold and Silver. Austin, Texas: American Atheist Press, 1990.

_____. Ethiopia and the Origin of Civilization. Baltimore: Black Classics Press, 1990.

_____. Introduction to African Civilizations. Secaucus, NJ: The Citadel Press, 1970.

James, Portia P. The Real McCoy. Washington, DC: Smithsonian Institution Press, 1989.

Kaplan, Sidney. Black Presence in the Era of the American Revolution 1770-1800. Washington, DC: New York Graphics Society, Ltd., 1973.

Katz, William L. Black Indians. New York: Atheneum, 1986.

Keen, Benjamin and Mark Wasserman. A History of Latin America. Boston: Houghton Mifflin, 1988.

Kramer, Ann, Lindy Newton, eds. Quest for the Past. Pleasantville, NY: The Readers Digest Association, Inc., 1984.

Lewis, David Levering. The Race to Fashoda. New York: Weidenfeld and Nicolson, 1987.

Logan, Rayford W. and Michael Winstons (eds.). Dictionary of American Negro Biography. New York: W.W. Norton Company, 1982.

Low, W. Augustus, Virgil A. Clift (eds.). Encyclopedia of Black America. New York: Da Capo. 1981.

Maunder, Samuel. The Treasury of History Volumes I and II. New York: Harper and Brothers, 1850.

Mokhtar, G. (ed.). Ancient Civilizations of Africa. Paris: UNESCO, 1990.

Morison, Samuel Eliot. Admiral of the Ocean Sea. Boston: Little Brown, 1942.

Morris, Richard B. (ed.). Encyclopedia of American History. New York: Harper and Row Publishers, 1961.

Norwich, Oscar I. Maps of Africa. Johannesburg: A.D. Donker, 1983.

Parr, Charles McKew. Ferdinand Magellan, Circumnavigator. New York: Thomas Y. Crowell, 1964.

Riley, James. An Authentic Narrative of the Loss of the American Brig Commerce. Hartford, CT. Judd Loomis and Company, 1836.

Rogers, Joel A. Africa's Gifts to America. St. Petersburg, FL: Helga M. Rogers, 1961.

_____. Sex and Race Volume II. New York: Helga M. Rogers, 1972.

_____. World's Great Men of Color, Volumes I and II, New York: Collier Books, 1972.

Roucek, Joseph S. (ed.) and Thomas Kiernan. The Negro Impact On Western Civilization. New York: Philosophical Library, 1970.

Rusco, Elmer R. Good Time Coming? Black Nevadans in the Nineteenth Century. Westport: Greenwood Press, 1985.

Shillington, Kevin. History of Africa. New York: St. Martin's Press, 1989.

Snowden, Jr., Frank. Blacks in Antiquity. Cambridge, MA, Harvard University Press, 1970.

Strayer, Joseph R. Hans W. Gatzke, E. Harris Harbison. The Course of Civilization. New York: Harcourt, Brace and World, 1961.

Tacitus, The Annals of Rome. Michael Grant, trans. London: Penguin, 1979.

Thacker, John Boyd. Christopher Columbus: His Life, His Work, His Remains. New York: G.P. Putnam and Son, 1903.

Torr, Cecil. Ancient Ships. Cambridge: Cambridge University Press, 1894.

Unwin, Raymer. The Defeat of John Hawkins. London: Allen and Unwin, 1961.

Van Sertima, Ivan, ed. African Presence in Early Europe. New Brunswick: Transaction Books, 1986.

_____. Blacks In Science Ancient and Modern. New Brunswick: Transaction Books, 1986.

_____. They Came Before Columbus. New York: Random house, 1976.

Wallechinsky, David and Irving Wallace. The People's Almanac No. 3. New York: Bantam Books, 1981.

Watts, Daud Malik. The 100,000 Horsemen of West Africa. Washington, DC: Afro-Vision, Inc., 1986.

_____. Black Presence In the Lands of the Bible. Washington, DC: Afro-Vision, Inc., 1990.

West, John Anthony. The Traveler's Key to Ancient Egypt. New York: Alfred A. Knopf, 1988.

Williams, Eric. From Columbus to Castro: The History of the Caribbean 1492-1969. New York: Vintage Book, 1984.

Wilson, Elinor. Jim Beckwourth. Norman: University of Oklahoma Press, 1988.

Windrow, Martin, ed. (Text by Terence Wise). Armies of the Carthaginian Wars 265-146 B.C. London: Osprey Publishing, 1985.

Woodson, Carter G. and Charles H. Wesley. The Negro In Our History. Washington, DC: The Associated Publishers, 1972.

Wright, Helen and Samuel Rapport. The Great Explorers. New York: Harper and Brothers, 1957.

Periodicals

Blackett, Richard, "Martin Delany and Robert Campbell: Black Americans in Search of an African Colony." Journal of Negro History, Vol. LXII, No. 1, January 1977, p. 38.

Fleming, Robert E. "Black, White and Mulatto" in Martin R. Delany's 'Blake': "Negro History Bulletin." Vol. 36. No. 2, February 1973, p. 12.

Gibbs, C.R. "Black Emperors of Rome." Metropolitan Magazine. Baltimore, MD, Vol. 5, No. 1, March 1979, p. 28.

Robins, Guy. "While the Woman Looks On: Gender Inequality in New Kingdom Egypt." KMT, A Modern Journal of Egypt, Vol. 1, No. 3. Fall 1990, p. 27.

Senerin, Timothy. "The Passion of Hernando De Soto." American Heritage Magazine. Vol. XVIII, No. 3, April 1962, p. 26.

The Salem Gazette. 20 September 1803 and 10 December 1805.

Miscellaneous Publications

Gibbs, C.R. Black Explorations of Mexico and the American West (Unpublished Manuscript), Washington, DC, 1974.

Van Sertima, Ivan, "Challenging the Columbus Myth" Congressional Testimony, July 7, 1987.

Picture Credits

Index

Biographical Note

Mr. C. R. Gibbs is an author, freelance writer, lecturer and exhibitor of historical artifacts. His many accomplishments include video scripts on Black History for the D.C. Public Schools Educational Media Center, a television script for a historical program on WETA and several scripts for WHUR-FM. He conducted research on Black Civil War units for the Sons of Union Veterans Organization, served as assistant technical advisor to the Frances Thompson Company on a film entitled "American Years" and as a consultant to the D.C. Public School System, Georgetown University, and the Smithsonian Institution. Mr. Gibbs is also a D.C. Community Humanities Council Scholar. He wrote, researched, and narrated "Sketches In Color," a 13-part companion series to the PBS series "The Civil War" for WHMM-TV, the Howard University TV station.

Mr. Gibbs has written for the Negro History Bulletin, American Visions, The Washington Post, The Washington Times, Dollars and Sense, The Baltimore Evening Sun, Sepia Magazine and several military publications. His articles have appeared in newspapers across the nation. Mr. Gibbs' research is cited in the official history of the United States Department of Commerce, *From Lighthouses to Laserbeams*. He is the author of several books entitled, *The Afro-American Inventor*, and *Friends of Frederick Douglass*, a children's book. *Black Georgetown Remembered*, his third book, he co-authored with Dr. Kathleen Lesko and Dr. Valerie Babb.

He has also lectured or exhibited historical items at the Martin Luther King, Jr. Memorial Library; the Frederick Douglass Memorial Home; Howard University, Northern Virginia Community College, University of Maryland, Towson State University; Loyola University; American University; public and private schools throughout the District of Columbia, Maryland and Virginia; the John F. Kennedy Center for the Performing Arts; the U.S. Merchant Marine Academy; Ft. Benjamin Harrison; and the National Archives.